PULPIT PLEADINGS

Other Books by the Author

From Feet to Fathoms
Lord, I Believe
Beds of Pearl
Whirlwinds of God

PULPIT PLEADINGS

By

ROBERT G. LEE

Pastor of Bellevue Baptist Church,
Memphis, Tennessee

Broadman Press

NASHVILLE, TENNESSEE

Broadman Press
Nashville, Tennessee

Printed in the United States of America
5D473

CONTENTS

I

Remembering the Words of Jesus

And they remembered his words.—LUKE 24:8.

In this text we are made to think of the functioning of man's memory, of Christ, of Christ's words.

Many are the manifestations of the efficient functioning of man's memory. We speak of the wonder of Blind Tom's memory. Blind Tom, the Negro boy, was a historic case of a phonographic mind without mentality. He could play from memory, after hearing it once, any piece of music, no matter how difficult. He could repeat in many languages speeches that he had heard, but he made his own thoughts known in grunts. He could play five thousand of the greatest classics in music, but he never felt any of them any more than the piano on which he played. That is a wonder of remembering.

Let us think of the

I. WONDER OF WORDS

We ask, What is a violet? and the poet answers, "A violet is a piece of perfumed floral velvet plus the solar system." We ask, What is a lump of coal? and the scientist answers, "A clot of the sun's blood turned black." We ask, What is a blade of grass? and the mystic says, "A blade of grass is an emerald harp string on which the bugling spring wind plays a resurrection melody."

We ask, What is spring? and somebody answers, "The time when cosmic tides break into billows of blossoms." We ask, What is a thunderstorm? and a child wisely answers, "God at his organ." We ask, What is the universe? and one answers, "A place in which a lot of love is better than much money." We ask, What is love? and the Bible says, "God is love." And another says, "The power which fertilizes every faculty, unifies all noble ideals, harmonizes all true work and workers, sweetens the speech of all tongues, fulfils all noble prophecies, explains all martyrdom, transfigures all hopes—and in all of these never fails."

We ask, What is a word? and before we answer, we think of two thousand seven hundred and ninety-six languages of the world, of the fact that seven hundred thousand is approximately the number of English words, of the fact that it takes the average child several years to learn one thousand words, of some men who have from six thousand to thirty thousand words at their command. We think of monosyllabic words and multisyllable words, or simple words and profund words, and of the truth that "language is the Rubicon which no animal ever crossed." But the dictionary says that a word is "an articulate sound, or combination of sounds, expressing an idea"—"a constituent part of a sentence." And, thinking of the wonder of words, Adelaide Proctor said:

> I have known one word to hang star-like
> O'er a dreary waste of years,

And it only shone the brighter
Looked at through a mist of tears.

Wonderful the words of lisping babe, of gladsome childhood, of vigorous and jubilant youth, of mumbling old age! Wonderful the words that come from the orator's mouth—like flights of golden arrows. Wonderful the words that come from the writer's pen—like golden pollen falling from the stems of shaken lilies. Wonderful the words that come from the singer's lips—building vocal palaces of melody and song.

Many times we have been taught that bodies die, but words live. When, in these recent years, Mars walked with bloody boots across the world and around the world, tying crepe to millions of doorknobs, covering the earth with the brains and blood and bones of slaughtered millions, it was in large part the result of the hysterical words of Hitler—words which brought about the Third Reich. We know that words have made possible the freedom of man, made beautiful many unknown things. Words tell of love between men and women. Words speak of God, of worship, of hatred, of misery, of death. Words can call for the uplift of a world—as did the words of Christ. Words can call for the destruction of nations—as did the words of Hitler.

Because of his use of words, Patrick Henry was called "the Tongue of the Revolution."

Because of his use of words, this was said of Henry Clay: "He had the faculty of crowding, as by some hydrostatic pressure of oratory, an amazing weight of expression on the backbone of a single word."

Because of his use of words, this was said of Daniel Webster: "His words were a song of triumph from the lips of one whose feet were on the beautiful mountains of the Promised Land."

Because of his use of words, this was what a newspaper man said of Henry Grady: "He managed in twenty minutes to bathe two antagonistic sections in fraternal light."

Because of the wild abandon in his use of words, this was said of Sergeant S. Prentiss: "He was the most wonderful speciman of sententious fluency."

Jack Kofoed recently wrote: "Written words are the ones that hold the history, the beauty, the courage and devotion of the past. They tell the tale, and point the finger. But the words we speak to each other can be oil or the sand in the fears of our existence. If they are words of brotherhood and understanding, the sun shines. If they are words of hatred and distrust, the cold wind blows, and the skies are dark."

But no words are adequate to portray the

II. Wonder of Jesus

A woeful sense of inadequacy oppresses the mind of any man who attempts with words of the mouth to proclaim Jesus, in the dignity of his person, in the glory of his character, in the condescension of his grace, in the wonders of his love, in the efficacy of his suffering, in the prevalence of his intercession, in the ability to save unto the uttermost those who come unto God by him.

Coequal, coexistent, coeternal, coessential with the Father is he. In eternity he rested on the bosom of the Father without a mother. In time he rested on the bosom of a mother without a father. In him we see that God, in Eden, brought a motherless woman from the body of a man—in Bethlehem brought a fatherless man from the body of a woman, and the Ancient of Days became the infant of days. He who "made all things in creation" (John 1:3) was "made flesh" to provide salvation. He who "made the law" was "made under the law." He who was "clothed with honor and majesty" was "wrapped in swaddling clothes." He who made woman was "made of a woman." He who was in "the form of God" was found "in fashion as a man"—and "as a man divine omnipotence moved in his arm, divine wisdom was cradled in his brain, divine love throbbed in his heart, divine compassion glistened in his eyes, divine grace poured from his lips, divine mercy wrought in human hands, divine holiness was manifested in the human walk, divine fulness dwelt in a human body."[1]

This is he whom God hath highly exalted and hath given a name which is above every name. This is he who was "once on a tree, but now on a throne—once in the place of humiliation, now in the place of exaltation—once in the place of degradation, now in the place of glorification—once in the place of debasement, now in the place of dignity—once in the place of wrath, now in the place of worship—once in the place of the curse, now in the place of the crown"[2]—once in the place of hellish horror, now in the place of heavenly honor. He stands august, supreme, unique. As Haldeman puts it: "There never was anything like him before. There never has been anything like him since. He is as a white rose surrounded by scarlet poppies—as a smile of love against a scowl of hate, as a song above discord, as a shaft of light in the

[1]Dr. Robert L. Moyer, pamplet published by Bruce Publishing Company, Twin Cities, Minn.
[2]Ibid.

blackness of a starless night.'"[3] But the best we can say of him is as man's mean paint on God's fair lilies.

But we are to think in remembrance and hold in remembrance the

III. Wonderful Words of Jesus

In Jesus' words his ideals are mirrored in everlasting brightness; in them he searches the depths; in them he draws pictures from mount and vale; in them he places upon the stage prophet and priest and king; in them he unfolds the life of beggar and slave; in them he descends into the dark depths of the grave; in them he descends to the doleful depths of hell; in them he goes into heaven and brings forth archangel and angel to act out the picture of his will.

Turn the microscope upon the words of Jesus. The severest ordeal has not discredited them. Scientists celebrate the skill of the Belgian chemist who eliminated from his chemicals every trace of that pervasive element, sodium, so thoroughly that even its spectroscopic detection was impossible. Far more wonderful the words of Jesus which, for boldness of conception, for grandeur of character, for valiant propagandism claim the sovereignty of the world—words which are diamonds in which there is no flaw; rivers whose sands are gold, whose depths glass the purity of the heavens and in which is no trace of mud; choirs in which there is no voice lifted in antithesis to the wisdom which is from above; declarations in which there is no trace of error or injustice; gardens in which no weeds mix with the flowers. And

---

[3]I. M. Haldeman, *Tabernacle Priesthood and Offerings* (New York: Fleming H. Revell Company) p. 38.

from him who illustrated in his daily life every doctrine of his heavenly mind we have this assurance: "Heaven and earth shall pass away, but my words shall not pass away."

Every word which Jesus spoke has been weighed and analyzed. For two thousand years they have been the object of intensive analysis. They have been the subject of unparalled investigations. His words have been torn into analytical pieces and thrust often into the laboratory of critical chemistry. They have been submitted to the cold and merciless investigation of Philistines of transcendent cleverness—tested thoroughly as to base, combination, compound parts—and even now are the object of iniquitous inspection. But has one accent been discovered as wrong? Has one emphasis been erroneous? Is one sentence or word in need of change? Can all men —searching, scrutinizing, sifting—find a single thought that ought to be reversed, or any statement that needs to be recalled?

Sometimes his words came with such softness, with gentle graciousness—sometimes with the note of distant thunder and the flash of flame in them, accompanied by a terrible light in his eyes—until the officers sent by his enemies to arrest him as one who disturbed public peace, were themselves arrested by the sound of his voice, by the accent of his words, by the marvelous measure of his thoughts. Therefore, they went back to those who sent them and said, "Never man spake like this man" (John 7:46).

A soldier of the old Grand Army of the Republic wrote a letter to the famous Henry Ward Beecher, pastor of Plymouth Church, requesting a copy of a prayer which the preacher had delivered a short time before. The colorful reply is still in the archives of the G. A. R.:

"Peekskill, July 11, 1878.

"General H. A. Barnum, Grand Marshal.

"You request me to send you my prayer made on Decoration Day evening. If you will send me the notes of the oriole that whistled from the top of my trees last June, or the iridescent globes that came in by millions on the last waves that rolled on the beach yesterday, or a segment of the rainbow of last week, or the perfume of the first violet that blossomed last May, I will also send you the prayer that rose to my lips with the occasion and left me forever.

"I hope it went heavenward and was registered, in which case the only record of it will be found in heaven.
"Very truly yours, Henry Ward Beecher."

Just so would we find it impossible with words to describe the words of Jesus. For his words are like warm hands placed upon practical life. And all truths uttered in any and every realm find their rootage in the words of Jesus.

We need to think of a

IV. Sad Situation

Upon these disciples the blinding rain of terrible gloom had fallen. Dumb were they under the horrors of Golgotha. Stunned were they, having seen the cruelties of the cross. Death, whose only flowers are faded garlands on coffin lids, had trampled into lifeless dust the Rose of Sharon. Death, whose only music is the sob of broken hearts, had padlocked the mouth that so comfortingly had spoken to the sad. Death, whose only palace is a huge sepulcher, numbered him among his victims. Death, whose only light is the darkness of the tomb, had quenched the Light of the world. Death, whose only pleasure fountains are the falling tears of the world, had closed the eyes of him who wept over Jerusalem. Death, whose only gold is the grave's dust, had made his body a banquet for worms. Death, with skeleton hand, had written "Ichabod" on all his claims. Terrorized they were by the experiences of Calvary—its darkness, its venom, its earthquake, its blood, its death. Ultimately they were overwhelmed. Their white ship of hope had gone to pieces on that hidden rock named a tomb. It was here that all the spiritual sailors on life's sea had met their doom, and they themselves, despite all Jesus had said, despite all the miracles he had wrought, were caught in the final dismay and were as helpless as a fly in a spider's web, as confused as one who gropes in a dark underground passage. "Death is still king," they said, as they went to the sepulcher with their spices. "We had hoped that a new morning had broken over the hills of time, but our hope is vain and our despair is well-founded." But the hour struck when the radiant lily took the place of the grinning skull—when Death shrank back in his lair and yielded up his prey—when Jesus shattered death's empire of skulls, of skeletons, with one blow.

Why had the disciples missed the message of that significant and triumphant hour? For the reason that they had disbelieved or forgotten the words of Jesus—like many of us do. And then—"they remembered his words."

"They remembered his words."	There is your sunburst at midnight.
"They remembered his words."	There are your roses in December.
"They remembered his words."	There is your health after sickness.
"They remembered his words."	There is the music after the mournful monotony of jangling inharmony.
"They remembered his words."	There is the calm after the terrible tempest—the harbor after a stormy voyage.
"They remembered his words."	There is the victory after seeming defeat.
"They remembered his words."	There is your rain after the scorching drouth.
"They remembered his words."	There is the freedom after the prison house life.
"They remembered his words."	There is the emancipation after slavery.

It was "the operation of the law of Christianized memory." It was the vindication of the honor at stake in all of God's words and the authentication of the promise in the words of Jesus when, speaking in the upper room of the ministry of the Holy Ghost, he said:

But the Comforter, which is the Holy Ghost, whom the Father will send in my name, he shall teach you all things, and bring all things to your remembrance, whatsoever I have said unto you (John 14:26).

Today we need a must upon us as to remembrance of Christ's words. We must remember his

V. Words About God

It is but to water the lawn in the rainstorm to say that Jesus excels all teachers in subject matter. Somebody has told us that Socrates was a question box into which the pre-Christian centuries dropped their queries; that Plato was the wonderland of Roman dreams for all noble idealists; that Aristotle was an enclycopedia of the ancient world, and that his big mental fingers have relaxed their mistaken grasp of things but slowly; that Homer was a blind nightingale who even now sings the heroism of the ancient and faraway; that Dante was the solemn jailer of the Middle Ages and that he carried a key to the bottomless pit, as well as a key to the golden doors of heaven, and that when he blew his trumpet both devils and angels answered his call; that Shakespeare was humanity's fully accredited detective whose unerring imagination carried him into the haunted rooms of human life; that Newton found a multiuniverse, world on world, running not one second ahead of, and not one second behind, God's appointed schedule. Inventing a vast string called gravity, he "gave one end of it an intellectual toss into infinity, linked all systems together, and then, bringing end to end, he tied a knot in the invisible string relating the whole."

Indebted we are to all these servants of humanity. They have told us many things about the universe, many things about racial possibilities, and much of the wonder and beauty of the world. But the loftier range of knowledge pertains to God, the great Creator who inhabits eternity and dwells with those who are of a humble and contrite heart, upholding all things by the word of his power. The other day I chose this as a choice passage:

What is God like? What is his character? What is his purpose? Why is Calvary? Who am I—with mystery behind me, with weakness within me, with the grave before me, with eternity calling me? I want to know who besets me behind and before and is acquainted with all my ways—to whom the darkness and the light are both alike—who understands my thoughts afar off. Is he good? Is he wise? Is he loving? Is he willing to stoop to my littleness? Is he patient to endure my deficiencies? These are questions involving absolutely highest knowledge.

Plato had no satisfying answer for them. Confronted by them, Newton and Shakespeare and all philosophers are as little boys, with trousers rolled up and attempting to wade the Atlantic from shore to shore.

The difference in their teaching and Christ's teaching is the difference in a speculation and a revelation, in an inquiry and a declaration, in surmise and certainty, in groping and guidance. And Christ not only *gives* the answer; he *is* the answer. Remember his words!

We must remember his words about

VI. God's Care

God's care of the individual is often forgotten or not acknowledged. But listen to the words of Jesus:

And why take ye thought for raiment? Consider the lilies of the field, how they grow; they toil not, neither do they spin: and yet I say unto you, That even Solomon in all his glory was not arrayed like one of these. Wherefore, if God so clothe the grass of the field, which today is, and tomorrow is cast into the oven, shall he not much more clothe you, O ye of little faith? Therefore take no thought, saying, What shall we eat? or, What shall we drink? or, Wherewith shall we be clothed? (For after all these things do the Gentiles seek:) for your heavenly Father knoweth that ye have need of all these things (Matthew 6:28-32).

Sometimes we ignore this gracious truth—like folks who light candles in the daytime, saying "There is no sun." Sometimes we deny this gracious truth—like those who say no wind blows when the cyclone rages. We saunter jejunely along without Christian clearness and free vision, which is fatal to efficient spirituality.

But Christ, who never deals in vague and vapid generalizations, says that the very hairs of our heads are numbered. And Job declares that he counts all our footsteps.

Behold the fowls of the air: for they sow not, neither do they reap, nor gather into barns; yet your heavenly Father feedeth them. Are ye not much better than they? (Matthew 6:26.)

According to what Christ said, God knows your address, your joys, your needs, your hopes, your fears, your sorrows, your sins, your desires to be better. It is when men are ignorant of or deny Christ's words that the old preternatural terrors of the universe come out to haunt us—and life becomes an idiot's tale full of sound and fury, signifying nothing. When the disciples remembered his words, they forgot their own despair, their own defeat, their own fears. It is always so. When Christ comes, the un-Christly goes.

Remembering his words about God's care of the individual, we should in faith set forth on any road, no matter how rough—launch out into any seas, no matter how stormy—give our shoulders to any burden, no matter how heavy—singing as we go:

Be not dismayed, whate'er betide,
  God will take care of you;
Beneath His wings of love abide,
  God will take care of you;

God will take care of you,
  Thro' ev'ry day, O'er all the way;
He will take care of you,
  God will take care of you.

We must remember his words about

VII. His Cross

From that time forth began Jesus to shew unto his disciples, how that he must go unto Jerusalem, and suffer many things of the elders and chief priests and scribes, and be killed, and be raised again the third day (Matthew 16:21).

At the cross he died as the great Criminal of the universe—as one who was made sin, as the Second man bearing the evil which was potentially in the first man. There, in overwhelming judgment, the agony of which he portrays through the lips of Jeremiah in the statement, "Behold, and see if there is any sorrow like unto my sorrow, . . . wherewith the Lord hath afflicted me in the day of his fierce anger"—the wrath of God, the antipodes of light to darkness, swept down upon him, and he was swallowed up in the anguish of eternal judgment, crying out as the heavens turned black and the earth reeled, "My God, My God, why hast thou forsaken me?"

We must remember his words about

VIII. Our Cross-Bearing

Then said Jesus unto his disciples, If any man will come after me, let him deny himself, and take up his cross, and follow me. For whosoever will save his life shall lose it: and whosoever will lose his life for my sake shall find it (Matthew 16:24-25).

In Forest Lawn Cemetery in Los Angeles, which strives to be a place of comfort without the hideous associations of death, there is a dedication which says, "There is no crucifixion in Forest Lawn." That may be all right there, but many have tried to do the same thing with life, saying "There is no crucifixion here!" If we are going with Jesus, there is one hill around which there is no detour. We cannot pick out triumphal entries and leave the crosses any more than we can pick out the sunshine and leave the rain. Cheap the concept of life as a crossless life. A life obsessed with saving itself from a cross will lose itself in nothingness. We hang the cross in gold about our necks, and we set it to flash in the sunlight on the steeples of our churches. But we must make it an experience in our lives.

We must remember and proclaim his words about the

IX. New Birth

"Ye must be born again."

There should be no marvel with the necessity of the new birth. We cannot understand the mystery of the natural birth, but we do not marvel at its necessity if we are going to live in this physical world. All who live in this world must be born into it. All who live in the spiritual world must be born into it, for there is no other way of getting into it; so marvel not about it.

When Whitefield, who preached over three hundred times on the new birth, was asked why he preached so often on it, he said: "Because 'ye must be born again.'" To have a Christian world, we must have Christians; and we do not have Christians until men are born again.

We must remember and put into practice—being doers of the Word and not hearers only—his words about

X. Fishing for Men

Now as he walked by the sea of Galilee, he saw Simon and Andrew his brother casting a net into the sea: for they were fishers. And Jesus said unto them, Come ye after me, and I will make you to become fishers of men (Mark 1:16-17).

Are you a worthy member of that ancient and honorable order of fishermen, founded by the Master on the shores of Lake Galilee when he said: "Come ye after me, and I will make you to become fishers of men"? This is the most imperative and inspiring task of the Christian. He must cast the line. He must dangle the rod. Else the devil's devotees will scoop the pool or dredge the depths—compassing sea and land to make proselytes for hell. Not harpooners can we be and go after Leviathans of the deep as did Moses, Elijah, John the Baptist, Luther, Knox—who stood before kings and smote them with the Word of God. Neither can we be netters as were Peter, Paul, and Moody—whose nets "nearly broke with the multitude of fishes." But we can all be linesmen, like Jesus, who, in the quiet pools of Sychar, Bethesda, and elsewhere caught solitary souls as an example of personal evangelism.

If we remember the words of Jesus, we will not be guilty of singing "Rescue the Perishing" while our rescue work is lacking in concern—making our practice perjure the words of our mouths. "Rescue the perishing, care for the dying" will be short meter poetry transposed into long meter activity. Often our Christian zeal is like someone said of Mr. Wordsworth's poetic powers:

"He sometimes made his poetic eagle do the work of a clucking hen." As a consequence of such, many unsaved around us say, "No man cared for my soul. Would that it could be said of all our members in all our churches what was said of Mr. Wesley: "He was out of breath pursuing souls." The seeking of a single individual by an individual has been God's chosen way of evangelism from the beginning of the Christian age. But too many of us are like the Italian coast guard who reported a wreck to the Government: "We attempted to give every assistance possible through the speaking trumpet—notwithstanding which, next morning twenty corpses were washed ashore." There is such a thing as being in this soul-winning business what Sir Walter Raleigh calls "lavish in words and niggard in deed."

Tangled in nets
Of our wild philosophy,
Caught in the backlash
Of ideas ill cast,
Heaving the lead
Into unplumbed infinity,
Baffled, we stand
Beside the shore at last.
Snagged barbs, snarled lines,
Torn sails! What fishers we!
O Man of Galilee![4]

Selecting good tackle, throwing out well, changing our lines when necessary, forgetting not the sinker of prayer lest our lines float lightly, fishing not with tangled lines, being not disappointed with small fish, distressed never over queer specimens, let us fish for folks—remembering that we cannot get results from the rocking boat of human philosophy, or the shifting sands of theological speculation, or the drifting launch of modernism that has lost its moorings.

There is a characteristic story of General Booth, founder of the Salvation Army, in the recently published memoirs of the late Rudyard Kipling. Once while touring the British Empire, Kipling met General Booth: "I saw

[4]Albert Reginald Gold, "Fishers," *1000 Quotable Poems* (Chicago: Willett, Clark and Company.)

him walking backward in the dusk over the uneven wharf, his cloak blown upwards, tulip fashion, over his grey head while he beat a tambourine in the face of the singing, weeping, praying crowd who had come to see him off. I talked much with General Booth during that voyage. Like the young ass I was, I expressed my distaste of his appearance at the wharf. 'Young feller,' he replied, bending great eyebrows at me, 'if I thought I could win one more soul to the Lord by walking on my head and playing the tambourine with my toes, I'd—I'd learn how!' "

Therein perhaps lies the secret of the success that has attended the efforts of the Salvation Army. It was this consuming desire to give God all that he had of himself, to place Christ and the interests of his kingdom first in his life, to be, if the occasion demanded, a fool for Christ's sake—it was these, we say, that brought divine blessing upon the efforts of that great man.

It is these same factors that today are needed to awaken a complacent, comfortable church to the realities of the gospel. Look back over the record of the Christian church and it will be found that the men and women who have done great things for God have been people of one aim and purpose and dominated by an all-consuming passion for the souls of men. When we really get the vision of a world that is dying without Christ, of men and women passing into a hopeless eternity apart from his remedial work upon the cross, then it may be there will arise others like Booth who will lay their lives completely down at the foot of the cross, take hold upon God and turn the world upside down.

"I will make you fishers of men." Believe heartily, accept joyfully, cling enthusiastically to the truth that when we are winning souls we are engaged in the greatest work that ever moved God's heart in compassion and his arm in power, that ever stirred an angel's wing in flight, that ever exacted tribute from the talents of men and women, that ever caused rejoicing in the presence of the angels of God. The Christian who does not see that, though he carry the epitome of all laboratories and observations within his single head is, as Carlyle would express it, "but a pair of spectacles behind which there is no eye."

We must remember the words of Jesus about

XI. Hell and Heaven

And fear not them which kill the body, but are not able to kill the soul: but rather fear him which is able to destroy both soul and body in hell (Matthew 10:28).

We dare not look upon his words concerning hell as something allegorical, metaphorical, poetical, or as a flagrant contradiction to the goodness of God. If hell is not fire, it is as severe as fire; and if it is as severe as fire, it had just as well be fire.

Watkinson says: "Although the New Testament is renounced, sin, devils, judgments, hell remain potential in the human conscience. To take away hell is to reject the physician and leave the plague, to overthrow the lighthouse and leave the hidden rock, to wipe out the rainbow and leave the storm, to take away the fire light and leave the fire to rage, to take away the vaccine and leave the smallpox. To take away hell is to meet the tragic blackness of sin with a candle gospel, to make a mild twilight out of eternal retribution, to take away the trumpet and open the gate to the enemies, to take away roses and leave the thorns, to throw away gold and press bankruptcy upon human life.''

As did Torrey, as did Moody, as did Spurgeon, as did Carroll, we must believe the old-fashioned Bible doctrine regarding hell. Hell is a logical necessity.

But as we believe that and preach that, let us not forget to believe and preach the *antithesis* of that—heaven!

Heaven, where no toil shall fatigue God's redeemed ones. Heaven, where no hostility can overcome them. Heaven, where no temptations can assail them. Heaven, where no pain can pierce them. Heaven, where no night can shadow them. Heaven, the most beautiful place the wisdom of God could conceive and the power of God could prepare.

Heaven, the land where they never have any heartaches, where no graves are ever dug. Heaven, where there is no hand-to-hand fight for bread. Heaven, where no hearse rolls its dark way to the tomb. Heaven, where David is triumphant, though once he bemoaned Absalom. Heaven, where Abraham is enthroned who once wept for Sarah. Heaven, where Paul is exultant, though once he sat with his feet in the stocks. Heaven, where John the Baptist is radiant with joy though he had his head chopped off in the dungeon. Heaven, where Savonarola wears a crown, though once he burned at the stake. Heaven, where Latimer sings praises, though once he simmered in the fire. Heaven, where many martyrs sit in the presence of Jesus, though their blood once reddened the mouths of lions. Heaven, where many saints rest in peace who once were torn on racks of torture.

Let us remember the words of Jesus about

XII. Prayer

Jesus said, "Pray ye!" The prayerless life is lacking in power. No spiritual power is existent apart from prayer. Prayer changes things within and without. Charles H. Spurgeon felt the need of a great auditorium where the people of London could come to hear the gospel preached. His deacons, more than thirty in number, did not believe that such a building could be built by a church without wealth. Spurgeon never wavered. He called all the deacons together, told them what he believed God wanted the church to do, and then asked all who doubted that it could be done to leave the meeting and those who believed it could be done to remain. Only six remained. They prayed through to victory.

A few days after the meeting, Spurgeon received notice from a bank that eighty thousand dollars had been deposited to the credit of the building fund of the church. He knew that God sent the gift in answer to prayer, but he never learned the name of the human messenger who made the deposit.

The greatest need in Christendom today is praying Christians. If we go forward and upward, we will do so on our knees.

> Wilt thou not revive us again,
> That thy people may rejoice in thee?

Dr. Jowett, of fragrant memory, once remarked: "I'd rather teach one man to pray than ten men to preach."

We should remember the words of Jesus about

XIII. Inward Purity

"Thou blind Pharisee, cleanse first that which is within the cup and platter that the outside of them may be clean also" (Matthew 23:26).

Woe unto you, scribes and Pharisees, hypocrites! for ye are like unto whited sepulchres, which indeed appear beautiful outward, but are within full of dead men's bones, and of all uncleanness. Even so ye also outwardly appear righteous unto men, but within ye are full of hypocrisy and iniquity (Matthew 23:27-28).

Which makes us to ask what Alexander Maclaren asks: "The rooms that look to the street are fairly clean. But what is there rotting and festering down in the cellars? Do we ever go down there with the candle of the Lord in our hands?" Which makes us also to think of Elizabeth Fry's indictment of herself once: "You are a contemptible small lady—all outside, no inside."

Remember his words—Oh, let us—about

XIV. His Coming Again

Which also said, Ye men of Galilee, why stand ye gazing up into heaven? This same Jesus, which is taken up from you into heaven, shall so come in like manner as ye have seen him go into heaven (Acts 1:11).

The second coming of Christ is the one event which, in the Scriptures, is always on the horizon, and, like the sunlight, it illumines all the theologic landscape with its glow and color.

From Genesis to Revelation this doctrine of the second coming is inwrought with the warp and woof of the inspired Word and lies as thick upon its pages as the autumn leaves which at this hour whirl in the woods; and he who keeps his ears alert as he opens its pages may hear the rustling of the footsteps of the coming King. The second coming is bound up with every fundamental doctrine of the Bible. The second coming is bound up with the doctrine of the resurrection. The second coming is bound up with the doctrine of divine sonship. The second coming is bound up with the deliverance of creation from the bondage of corruption. The second coming is bound up with the deliverance of God and Christ over Satan. The second coming is bound up with the recognition of the dead. The second coming is bound up with the exhortation to Christian living.

But Christ's reappearing is a certainty—by requirement. The great scheme of redemption requires his return. It is part of that scheme that as he came once with a sin offering, he should come a second time without a sin offering. As he came the first time to redeem, he must come a second time to claim the inheritance which he has so dearly bought. As he came once that his heel might be bruised, he comes again to break the serpent's head—and with a rod of iron to dash his enemies in pieces, as a potter's vessel. As he came once to wear the crown of thorns, he must come again to wear the crown of universal dominion. He comes to glorify his saints with himself on this same earth where once he and they were despised and rejected of men. As he came once as a Prince in disguise, to win the heart of the world by his lowliness and love, he will come again to be revealed in all his glory as King of kings and Lord of lords.

There are those who scoff and ask, "Where is the promise of his coming?" (2 Peter 3:4.) But you cannot ha-ha the song out of the mockingbird's throat. You cannot laugh the sun out of the sky. You cannot scoff the fragrance away from flowers. You cannot deride the morning star away. You cannot stop the rising sun with scorn. He is coming again! And his coming will be the watcher's looked-for day, the purchaser's redemption day, the builder's completion day, the husbandman's harvest day, the servant's recovery day, the master's payday, the Son's manifestation day, the bride's wedding day, the King's coronation day.

Therefore, let us pray with Richard Baxter:

> Hasten, O Master, the time of thy return.
> Delay not—lest the living give up their hopes.
> Delay not—lest the earth grow like hell.
> Delay not—lest our hearts faint.
> Delay not—lest wickedness triumph.

Oh, hasten that day when the graves which received but rottenness and retain but dust shall yield up the bodies of Christians in the first resurrection, to be glorified.

Let me ask you to remember the words of Jesus about the

XV. Worldwide Proclamation of the Gospel

"Go ye into all the world."

"Go ye." We ought to be a going concern for Jesus. "Go ye." I heard a drunk man, dying in jail, after trouble with his wife, thanking God he was holding his own! "Holding the fort." "Go ye"—not just to stand where you are. "God so loved the world." We are to go into all the world. "He is the propitiation for our sins: and not for ours only, but also for the sins of the whole world" (1 John 2:2). We are to make a public declaration of this great truth—making appeal to the hearts of men, not just going forth in philosophical argument to convince men's minds. If we will announce the great verities of the faith, as trumpeters that give no uncertain sound, God will bless. Isn't this the great thing we are called to do—simply and earnestly to announce the great truths of revelation—not to submit them for subdued discussion in academic grove?

So many want to organize something—get up more schemes of world change, some project of human betterment. But Jesus still says: "Go, preach the gospel." In the centuries gone forever into the tomb of time, the disciples did. And they "turned the world upside down," putting out the altar fires of Diana, taking the hinges off the doors of resisting kingdoms, storming the capitals of proud empires in the name of Jesus, leaving a trail of glory across the Gentile world, carrying the banner of the cross over a wider territory than the Roman eagles shadowed.

Thus we shall have the spirit which will give us victory over the world, the flesh, the devil—in life and in death.

Dr. Ray A. Petty, once pastor of the First Baptist Church in Kansas City, Missouri, was successor to Dr. Russel H. Conwell at the great Baptist Temple of Philadelphia. Dr. Beaven tells of his victorious life and victorious death:

"Dr. Petty died at the age of forty-five, after a life of outstanding unselfishness, having dedicated himself to the service of his fellow men with an enthusiasm and an indifference to self that is seldom matched. He suffered all through mature life with a heart difficulty that had resulted from a sickness in his youth. When in the later years other complications arose, his depleted physical reserve proved unable to stand the strain. The closing moments before he went are an imperishable memory to all who knew him. His mind was clear. His triumphant spirit was in full vigor. Toward the sunset hour of that eventful day he noticed the nurses, the doctor, and his wife were all in the room. He seemed to sense that something was impending. Turning to the doctor, who was his close personal friend, he said, 'Walter, tell me, am I going to go?' And the doctor, conscious that nothing but the absolute truth would be a fair answer, replied, in a voice hard to control because of its emotion, 'Yes, Ray, it is your time to go.' In the face of that terrific moment came the exhibit of the triumphant power of a great objective in life to which I have referred. Taking the hand of his wife and the hand of his doctor, and bowing in prayer, he lifted them, and his children, and the interests to which he had committed himself, before God in words that melted the hearts of all who listened. Then, lifting himself with his last bit of strength, and raising his arm to salute, he said: 'The records are all in. I'll soon be with Mother and Wallace. And when I do go, I'll walk straight unto the gates of heaven and say, as I salute, "Lord, I'm ready for the next task.'"

"That is living 'after the power of an endless life.' It is being part of a great on-going enterprise. It is marching on a trail that does not run into a cul-de-sac called the grave. Such a spirit changes the grave from a dead-end street into a far-stretching highway on which one travels across the long years of eternity."[5]

---

[5]Dr. Beaven, *Sermons for Everyday Living* (Philadelphia: The Judson Press) pp. 93-94.

NOTE.—Delivered before the Tennessee State Baptist Convention, on November 12, 1946.

II

Widened Reach and Heightened Power

Enlarge the place of thy tent, and let them stretch forth the curtains of thine habitations: spare not, lengthen thy cords, and strengthen thy stakes.—ISAIAH 54:2.

As I speak upon this subject, I would mention five words upon which I would ask you to pitch your mental tents—prayerfully and heart-searchingly: worth, wisdom, wonder, world, work.

We think of the

I. WORTH

This word points us to Isaiah, worth much to God and to God's purposes of grace—Isaiah, who, by the Holy Spirit, wrote the words of our text. "Isaiah the son of Amoz." "The Lord said, . . . My servant Isaiah" (Isaiah 20:3). "Spake the Lord by Isaiah" (Isaiah 20:2). Isaiah—mouthpiece of God. Isaiah serving God—and sometimes spectacularly sensational in service. To that truth these words testify:

And the Lord said, Like as my servant Isaiah hath walked naked and barefoot three years for a sign and wonder upon Egypt and upon Ethiopia; so shall the king of Assyria lead away the Egyptians prisoners, and the Ethiopians captives, young and old, naked and barefoot, even with their buttocks uncovered, to the shame of Egypt (Isaiah 20:3-4).

Isaiah, the evangelist among prophets, servant of the Lord, as was Jonah behind the curtain of whose preaching old Nineveh shifted scenes of riot for penitential tears.

Isaiah, servant of the Lord, whose dignity compelled priests to bow in his presence, even as Joseph was servant whose statesmanship wiped frowns from a tyrant's brow and whose spiritual insight and foresight took fear from the heart of a famine-smitten world.

Isaiah, servant whose voice, conscience strengthened, rocked thrones with terror even as Amos was a servant who, at a time when the scepter was frozen with the tyranny of impeached civilizations, summoned nations to judgment.

Isaiah, servant whose voice was often a succession of sobs in the night, even as Jeremiah, whose weeping resembled the weeping of a brokenhearted archangel over a lost world, was a servant of the Lord.

Isaiah, servant in whose preaching was the growl of the Assyrian wolf, even as Ezekiel was a servant, Ezekiel whose tears turned to blood as he listened to the rumbling wheels of oncoming destruction.

Isaiah, servant of God in whose preaching were the thunders of Sinai, even as Elijah, calling an apostate nation back to God, was servant of the Lord.

Isaiah, servant of the Lord, as was John the Baptist, who prepared the way for Jesus and to whom was given the delicate and sacred task of interpreting the voice of betrothal. "The voice of him that crieth in the wilderness, Prepare ye the way of the Lord, make straight in the desert a highway for our God" (Isaiah 40:3).

Isaiah, servant in whose preaching were the foregleams of Calvary, even as Moses was servant—Moses who formulated a ceremonial system which expresses faith in God, sacrifice for sin, atonement for reconciliation, and "the moral element which forms the background of the cross."

Isaiah, servant of the Lord, as was Paul who left a trail of glory across the Gentile world and compassed the earth with the truths of redemption.

Isaiah, servant, as was the prophet Samuel, who washed the heart of Israel with the snow of high ideals.

Isaiah, whom God called "my servant."

Isaiah, by whom God spake.

Isaiah, who said: "That which I have heard of the Lord of hosts, the God of Israel, have I declared unto you" (Isaiah 21:10).

These truths about Isaiah urge us to be people who possess what we profess; people who for God weigh sixteen ounces to the pound, measure thirty-six inches to the yard, and strike twelve; people whose shining for God before men is not as a spluttering candle flickering in the wind but as a steady lamp "trimmed and bright with undiminished and unfailing burning"; people who for God are not pewter but pearl, not calico but silk, not tawdry tinsel but genuine gold; people who are not mere pledgers but performers; people who are not mere hearers only but doers of the word; people who, seeking to be "perfect unto every good work," pass from the desire to the deed, pass from the idea to the reality; people who are not paste jewels but rare gems; people who are not content with a conventional Christianity, but, reaching forth to larger ambitions, seek to be worth all we should be *to* our God and *for* our God.

Surely if Christ once had need of a donkey (Luke 11:3) for his official presentation of himself as King, God has need of us to prove by good works that there are more excellencies in the performance of the duties of a plain Christian than in all the triumphs and glories of Caesar and Alexander. Surely since, in the long ago, Jesus used a lad's lunch of five loaves and two fishes (Matthew 14:17) to feed thousands, he will use us to be "eyes to the blind, and feet to the lame" (Job 29:15). Surely, as once by the shores of Galilee he made a pulpit of a ship (Mark 4:1), he will daily make us channels through which the divine shall become articulate.

Now, think about the word

II. Wisdom

It is wisdom to make real the figure herein found—the enlargement of the tent, the lengthening and strengthening of the cords, the stretching forth of the curtains expansively, and strengthening the stakes mightily. It is not wisdom to give heed to the voice that says:

> No farther shoot
> Thy broad ambitions bands,
> Contract thy firmament
> To the compass of a tent.

It is wisdom to believe that God is a God of enlargement, enlarging us by his plans above and beyond our plans as the oak is enlarged above the acorn in strength;

as the eagle is above and beyond the sparrow in flight; as the river is enlarged above the rill in reach; as the blossom is enlarged above the bud in fragrance; as, for purposes of habitation, a house of many rooms is enlarged above and beyond a cabin of two rooms; as, for travel purposes, a highway is beyond a mountain trail.

The psalmist said: "And hast not shut me up into the hand of the enemy: thou hast set my feet in a large room" (Psalm 31:8). Also, "I called upon the Lord in distress: the Lord answered me, and set me in a large place" (Psalm 118:5).

How great the folly of those who, answering no challenge to enlargement, say:

> I ponder not the farthest reach
> Of yon infinitude, the sea,
> Those ripples on the silver beach
> Trace wonders vast enough for me.

It is wisdom to remember that there is that which brings leanness of soul; to remember that "the soul grows fat only on immensities, infinities, eternities" and that "life clothes itself in the most vigorous realities only in altitudes, magnitudes, infinitudes."

We shall be wise to remember, as we give thought to the figure of the tent, the curtains, the cords, the stakes, that the curtains are the promises and provisions of the gospel; that those curtains will stretch as wide as the needs of human lives; that the cords are the cords of Christian graces and Christian effort and Christian service; that the cords need to be long—and as strong as they are long, and strong all the way along from end to end; for the maxim in physics has a spiritual application here

—teaching us that the cord is no stronger than its weakest place. We should ever hold in mind that our efforts for Christ's kingdom causes and objectives should have a wider reach; for God has committed unto us the work of reconciliation—the gospel in its fulness. Never, at any time or at any place, must we preach ourselves, "but Christ Jesus the Lord and ourselves your servants for Jesus' sake." Yet "we have this treasure in earthen vessels, that the excellency of the power may be of God, and not of us" (2 Corinthians 4:7). And we must feel every hour of every day the necessity to be "always bearing about in the body the dying of the Lord Jesus, that the life also of Jesus might be made manifest in our body. For we which live are alway delivered unto death for Jesus' sake, that the life also of Jesus might be made manifest in our mortal flesh" (2 Corinthians 4:10-11).

"For the grace of God that bringeth salvation hath appeared unto all men, teaching us that, denying ungodliness and worldly lusts, we should live soberly, righteously, and godly, in this present world, looking for that blessed hope, and the glorious appearing of the great God and our Saviour Jesus Christ; who gave himself for us, that he might redeem us from all iniquity, and purify unto himself a peculiar people, zealous of good works" (Titus 2:11-14).

This means that it is wisdom for us to remember that personal holiness is a prerequisite; for, as saith a wise man, God cannot trust an unsanctified people or an unconsecrated man or woman with service for him. But for service which will be well-pleasing unto him we must have wisdom—"the wisdom that is from above" which is "first pure, then peaceable, gentle, and easy to be intreated, full of mercy and good fruits, without partiality, and without hypocrisy" (James 3:17).

When we think of "widened reach and heightened power," we see that in many realms there is this

III. Wonder

We see the wonders of widened reach and heightened power in the scientific world and in the chemical realm —wonders that almost awake in us a primeval faith in magic—laboratory wonders that make *Andersen's Fairy Tales* seem prosaic prose. With the telegraph man has reached through and across vast distances to write—with heightened power. With the telephone man has reached across continents to talk with heightened power. With the phonograph man compressing a Caruso into the microscopic point of a needle and imprisoning choruses in wax discs, has reached into the dead years to enable us to hear the voices of people long dead. With the wireless telegraphy man has reached with heightened power across oceans separated by continents and over continents as wide as oceans. With that insulated thing called the cable, man has reached across oceans and beneath the surface of oceans mooring continents together. With the airplane man, in daring flight, has reached cloud regions, "out-eagling" the eagle. With the submarine man has reached into the ocean's depths. With the microscope man's eyes have reached into the infinitesimal worlds existent in a drop of blood or a drop of water. Man has turned mold into penicillin and atoms into earthquakes. With the telescope man has magnified the power of the human eye, enabling it, with widened reach and heightened power, to view landscapes of other worlds millions of miles away. With the spectograph man has reached the inside of planets great distances away and has discovered their constituent elements—the gold in the sun, the copper in Mars, and the iron on the moons of Jupiter. With antitoxins man has reached into the land of diseases and plague and has said: "Hitherto shalt thou come, but no further." With the radio we have made our ears reach to every corner of the globe and hear whispers. With chemical fingers we have reached into coal tar and have gotten out of it a substance five hundred times sweeter than sugar. With the X-ray we have reached down into the secret recesses of the human body—have looked beyond fleshly veils where none dare intrude with cheap scorn. With the incandescent light we have reached into regions of night and have made the blackest midnight glorious with auroral splendors.

Today we see in transportation facilities and in communication methods the wonders of "widened reach and heightened power." Jefferson voyaged to represent our nation at the Court of Paris with hardly more advantages of travel than Columbus enjoyed. News of Madison's election was three weeks in reaching Kentucky. No telling how long it was before it reached Arkansas and Texas! When Washington died on the banks of the Potomac, it was sixteen days before the people in Charleston, South Carolina, received the sad news. Once in our vast land mails and messages were speeded on their way as when David watched from Jerusalem's walls for news of his wild and wicked boy, Absalom. When Andrew Jackson was President of the United States, he wrote to a loved one at Nashville, Tennessee, saying: "We arrived in Washington last night at ten o'clock—

in good health but very much fatigued, because we travelled seventy miles in the two days"!

Recently I was out hunting amid the hills with one of my deacons. Glancing at the sky, we saw a huge "something like aluminum lightning" flit across the sky. Our eyes had to be swift to catch a glimpse of it! At least one mile behind it came a loud roar. We found out later that it was the jet plane which flew from Memphis to Nashville in twenty minutes. About three months later, I heard over the radio, even as later I read it in the newspaper, how, on April 21, 1946, Captain Martin L. Smith, Kidder, Missouri, flew a jet-propelled plane from New York to Washington in twenty-nine minutes—averaging four hundred and fifty miles an hour. The Associated Press, in its account, made this comment: "When the plane streaked over National Airport, it was going so fast the roar of its engine sounded a mile or so behind." This makes me think of the policeman who tried, but could not catch a Negro boy. He was asked why he couldn't catch him. The policeman replied with humiliation and seriousness: "Well, I tried, but the closer I got to him the farther he was away—and the last time I saw him he was clear out of sight!"

We see the wonder of "widened reach and heightened power" in so many achievements of inventive science. The old covered wagon that had a calendar for a timetable has been superseded by the far-reaching and complex systems of railroads. Heightened power! With the coming of the cotton gin in 1792, the little patches of white that had clung around the cabin door began to spread until they covered the Southland like snow. At the call of the cotton gin the idle streams—lazy vagrants

—were harnessed and made to turn myriads of spindles, the red hillsides were reared into factory walls, and the sleeping ore of the mountains was transformed into roaring machinery. Widened reach! Heightened power!

The old scythe, like those used by the Egyptians in the Nile Valley, like those used by the Babylonians in the valley of the Euphrates, have been thrown from the fields where now reapers "like yachts careen through fields of waving grain." Heightened power!

Water heated to two hundred and twelve degrees becomes steam. Heightened power! And if the steamer *Europa* obtained her motive power as the Spartan admiral, Eurybiades, obtained his at the Battle of Salamis, she would have to carry oarsmen to the number of three million men.

In King Alfred's day not one poor man in one thousand could read or write. But Gutenberg profoundly aroused civilization when he invented the movable type printing press. He gave the Bible to the people, and they rose to freedom and enlightenment from the serfdom and darkness of ages. Bible in hand, they leaped over the antique walls of civilization, destroyed prejudices rooted in the immemorial past, and that press widened the blind alley of ignorance into endless highways of wisdom. Widened reach and heightened power indeed!

Michael Faraday, scientist nonpareil, Christian superlative, serves millions even today through his inventive work in induction. In producing the dynamo, he directly hitched the wheels of industry to all our coal fields and waterfalls. Thus was, and is, the lawless torrent bridled and invested with power. Heightened power!

Where once the Indian, with bow and arrow, stalked wild animals in the woods, man, with Remington in hand and to shoulder, kills at a mile's distance. Widened reach and heightened power!

Men take chromium, a corrosion-resisting substance, and add seven-tenths of one per cent to low carbon steel and thus increase the tensile strength of that steel from fifty-five thousand pounds to the square inch to one hundred thousand pounds to the square inch. That is what the chemical scientist would call heightened power.

Once it was the spade; now it is the steam shovel. Once it was the needle; now it is the sewing machine. Once it was the bateau; now it is the ocean greyhound. Once it was the bellows; now the blast furnace. Once it was the kite; now it is the airplane. Once it was the milk jar; now it is the cream separator. Once it was the stairway; now the escalator and the hydraulic elevator. Once it was the goose quill pen; now the typewriter. Once it was the tinder box; now the safety match. Once it was the barn lantern; now the searchlight. Once the wheelbarrow; now the locomotive. Once the sledge hammer; now the pile driver. Once the washpot and clothesline; now the steam laundry. Once the keg of powder; now the atomic bomb. Cases all of heightened power!

Last March, the Western Cartridge Company, through the engineers of the company, disclosed development of a new superstop watch capable of recording velocity at 1/100000 (a hundred-thousandth) of a second—used to check bullet speeds. The clocking mechanism, employing an electronic counting system composed of tiny neon bulbs, starts counting when the first bullet passes over the first bulb of the circuit and stops when it passes the last. Electronic impulses tell the exact speed of the bullet. Heightened power in recording speed, that!

But I was asked to direct your thought and intensify your concern about "heightened power and wider reach in matters of world redemption." And that possessed, not just thought upon, not just talked about, means greater belief in and stronger effort for a wider circle than we ever dared dominate before. "Widened reach and heightened power" means elimination of passive acquiescence in small achievements—means no careless indifference to great stretches of the unattained—means no rolling of marbles when there should be removal of mountains.

Wider reach and heightened power means we make the world our parish, seeking to make the gospel known in its fulness in every hamlet of our own land and in every land and tongue. The tragedy of lessened power will be ours if we forget that God's Word is the first stake. The more widespread the work God gives us to do, the more important it is that we be true to the great standard of truth, the Bible, and to the gospel of Jesus Christ. This is the day of an undisciplined liberalism that goes nowhere so fast it arrives out of breath, telling us more and more of less and less. We will find ourselves with narrowed reach and lowered and lessened power if we succumb to the spiritual latitudes of today as wide as Sahara Desert and as correspondingly dry; if we ourselves are guilty of an intellectual recoil against anything emotional and see not the obvious inadequacy of rationalism as a substitute. We shall have lessened reach and lowered power if we preach not the Word—being instant in season and out of season—"reproving, rebuking, exhorting, with all longsuffering and doctrine."

Tragic, for ourselves and others, it will be if we narrow our reach and lessen our power by placing smug aestheticism above spiritual anxiety, brevity above burden-bearing, benevolence above blood, building above brotherliness, culture above conversions, criticisms above consolations, denouncement of others above denials of self, envies above excellencies, faintness above fervor, feeling above faith, goodness above grace, harangue above helpfulness, indifference above intensity and spiritual intoxication, jealousies above joy, jubilation above justification, kicking above kneeling, littleness above life, loading above love, the minimum above the maximum, the miserly above the missionary, the meticulous above the mighty, nevers above nows, overlordism above overwork, pep above prayer, play above purity, the palatable above the profitable, quarreling above quietness, reformation above regeneration, science above Scripture, sociability above spirituality, strife above service, theories above truth, tattling above testimony, uselessness above unction, vivacity above virtue, variance above vitality, words above work, zest above zeal, yarning and yawning above yearning.

Now let us consider the

IV. World

One does not have to be a photographer of sordid spots, nor a driver of a garbage wagon to say truthfully, if with sadness, that this is one mess of a world, a rotten world, whether looking around us, whether listening over the radio, whether reading newspapers, whether glancing over the news stands, whether attending the theaters, whether counting the liquor stores and beer barrels, whether observing the political pigmies where giants ought to be, whether attending some churches which have become "drifting sepulchres manned by frozen crews," whether coming in contact with what one college president calls "the poor products of our educational system," we have sympathy with the poet who wrote, whether in lamentation or cynicism, I know not:

> I vow, O God,
> Not for all the power furled and unfurled,
> Nor for all the temples to thy glory built,
> Would I assume the ignominous guilt
> Of having made such men in such a world.

We can say of our world what Shakespeare said:

> The world is grown so bad,
> That wrens make prey where eagles dare not perch.

What Horace wrote long ago describes our world:

> Wasting and a new troop of fevers
> Have settled upon the earth.

And we cannot with certainty deny what Byron wrote:

> The world is a bundle of hay,
> Mankind are the asses who pull;
> Each tugs it a different way.

And we agree with Walpole, who said:

> The world is a comedy to those who think—
> A tragedy to those who feel.

And Wordsworth spoke no foolishly descriptive words when he wrote:

> The fretful stir
> Unprofitable, and the fever of the world.

Yes, the world is sick and terribly disordered. Its debility is evident—and for this debilitation men have no medicine or surgery. The world is filled with anger and anguish. The world is filled with brutality and bestiality. The world is filled with clashing and cursing. The world is filled with doubt and despair and death. The world is filled with faithlessness and ferocity. The world is filled with godlessness and guilt. The world is filled with horribles and the harrowing. The world is filled with iniquity and intrigue. Everywhere we read of killings and kidnapings. Everywhere we read of lust and licentiousness. Everywhere we read of murder and maligning. Everywhere we read of nights of crime and days of debauching. Order has given away to disorder, and pleasure and pang and pain clutch at every life. Quarreling among men. Chasms across which men glare at one another in suspicion and ill will. Sorrow, suffering, and sin abound. Tragedy with its tears. Terror with its tragedies. War and wickedness have made a generation wild. Black snow falls. Sirocco winds from the devil's Sahara have burned the divine dew off the grass. Spiritual mercury has fallen low. There is the administration of laughing gas for the painless extraction of sin.

It is a day of invertebrate theology. It is a day of India-rubber convictions. It is a day of seesaw religion. It is a day of somersault philosophy. It is a day of semi-erroneous psychology. And when we think of the evil of legalized liquor traffic, we almost agree that this country is "the land of the spree and the home of the rave."

But, looking at this world, which has many religions but only one gospel, we must remember that God calls for a worldwide proclamation: "Go ye into all the world." We must remember that this worldwide proclamation is vitalized by a worldwide Presence: "I am with you." We must remember that this worldwide Presence is possessed of a worldwide power: "All power is given unto me in heaven and in earth." We must remember that this worldwide power is directed by a worldwide plan: "Go, preach, baptize, teach." We must remember that this worldwide plan contains a worldwide plea: "Look unto me, and be ye saved;" "believe on the Lord Jesus Christ." We must remember—and be encouraged by remembering—that this worldwide plea is accompanied by a worldwide promise: "My word shall not return unto me void." And we must remember that if our hearts are less than twenty-five thousand miles in circumference, they are too small. And we must guard ourselves against being found guilty by the words of Maltbie D. Babcock, who said: "Your love has a broken wing if it cannot fly across the sea."

All we have said brings us now to consider our

V. Work

What must be a reality if we enlarge the place of our tent? What must be our convictions if we stretch forth the curtains of our habitations? What must we be if we would lengthen our cords? What must we do if we would strengthen our stakes? What steps must we take to make continued advance and ceaseless aggression? What garments must we clothe ourselves in to enable us to march to worldwide victory—and be found faithful until the vanishing goals of time give place to the many mansions of the Father's House? How shall we live in the light of the urging of necessity for "widened reach and heightened power in world redemption?"

A British author recently wrote: "A perfectly sanitary, well-fed, well-clothed world without spiritual religion would be very much like an efficient and up-to-date zoo." Yes, a zoo—with chattering monkeys which say nothing, with squawking parrots, with growling bears, with raucous crows, with clamorous magpies, with roaring lions, with snarling tigers, with laughing hyenas, with coughing coyotes, with hissing serpents, with barking seals, with bellowing buffaloes, with quacking ducks, with greedy pelicans.

If we would do our work effectively—if we would avoid "tantalizing with vapours a world perishing of thirst"—if we would make real this enlargement of the tent, the stretching forth of the curtains, the lengthening of the cords, the strengthening of the stakes—if we show wisdom that will not expect this to be "by human mechanism or contrived instrument starting in ignorance and ending in selfishness"—there must be the right center, the wider our work the stronger it must be at the center. As the cords are lengthened, the stakes must be strengthened. We must be hottest at the center so that "the very ardour of the heat at the center shall be the outgoing rays of warmth and light and comfort until the whole circumference shall quiver, as with a palpitation of thankfulness." No circumference is strong with a weak center. No circumference of steel is held with spokes of straw that are fastened in a fragile spool hub. There is no strong wheel with a weak hub, a weak center. Oceans do not come from mudpuddles. Rivers do not run from cup reservoirs. If the sun were a candle, or if it were a sun of lessened power, less mighty, I wonder what the result on planets that circle it would be. Would Saturn,

885,000,000 miles away, going round the sun once in thirty years, be put out of place? Would Uranus, 1, 780,-000,000 miles away, going around the sun once every eighty years, at a speed of eighty miles an hour, be confused? Would Mars, 200,000,000 miles away, going around the sun once in six hundred and twenty-seven days, at a speed of forty-nine thousand miles an hour, be any different? The gravity of the earth is ever pulling every terrestrial object down to itself. The pulls are exerted in parallel lines—and the resultant of these parallel forces always passes through a point in the given object which is called the object's center of gravity. At this center of gravity, the whole mass of the body may be considered as concentrated. There is in the universe (astronomers say) some central sun around which all starry systems revolve—some given point where there is the centralization of the total mass of the universe.

Of greater importance is the question of the center of gravity of our Christian endeavors—as to just where the concentration of our beings, our thoughts, our words, our deeds may be. Shall we make sure that that center is the Christ of God and his cross—his cross where the history of human guilt culminates, where the purposes of divine love are made intelligible? Marvin says: "The cross, breaking the hellward fall of man, restores him to the true center of gravity in the celestial sphere." Believing that, we must remember that when we take Jesus and his cross as the center, all the radii of existence point to him and meet in him. Any other center is too small and too inglorious for all things to find a congenial and harmonious dwelling place. Forever is Jesus Christ the luminant center and interpreting principle of all in heaven and all in earth and all beneath the earth. Nothing and nobody except Jesus should we see on any mount of revelation, in any valley of ordinances, rites, ceremonies.

One of the greatest things ever said about the disciples who put out the altar fires of Diana and carried the banner of the cross over a pagan world was this: "The pressures of a hostile world never moved them from their center."

Speaking of the truth which we have just spoken, Dr. A. C. Dixon, with weighty words and wise, said: "If you can find a man in whom all truth is centered, not contending for the truth, but dying for those in error, you have reached another degree of glory. If you can find a man in whom all light is centered, light not displaying itself, but dying for those in darkness; if you can find a man in whom all wisdom is centered, not wisdom admiring itself, but dying for the ignorant; if you can find a man in whom all life is centered, not protecting itself, as a coward would, but giving itself for those who are dead; if you can find a man in whom all holiness is centered, holiness not cultivating itself, but giving itself on the altar, dying for the unholy and the impure; if you can find a man that has all power, not exerting itself, but willing to be weak; if you can find a man that is all love not simply enjoying itself, but love on the altar; love dying, love giving itself to the Cross in order that the unlovely might be saved; if you can find all these in one person you have some little conception of what the Cross of Christ means. Now put all into one—all Truth, Light, Life, Wisdom, Power, Holiness, Love incarnate in one man, who gives Himself for the untruthful, for the darkened, for the dead, for the weak, for the unholy, for the unlovely—and you have some conception of what the Cross of Jesus Christ is in its deeper meaning. That is our only center around which all must revolve."

If, in matters of preaching the gospel to all peoples, we would live up to the fulness of our possibilities, there must be the right conception of the church.

Christ is the Word. The church is the exponent of Christ. The church is the fruit in which he is glorified—even as the sun is glorified in fragrant and beautiful flowers. "Christ loved the church, and gave himself for it; that he might sanctify and cleanse it with the washing of water by the word, that he might present it to himself a glorious church, not having spot, or wrinkle, or any such thing; but that it should be holy and without blemish" (Ephesians 5:25-27).

Yes, Christ gave *himself* for the church. He gave his divinity to become incarnate. He did not reserve that. The church is everything to Christ. The church is "the fulness of him that filleth all in all" (Ephesians 1:23). Would not Christ, the God-man, be incomplete without the church? Can you imagine a Christ without a church? The conception would be absurd. And Christ is all in all to the church. Her being is consummated in him. Without him she is nothing. He is the supreme magnet of her desire. His strength is the joy of her weakness. His wisdom is the light of her ignorance. The majesty of his brow is the triumph of her love. The kingly tone of his commands elevates and ennobles her obedience. He is her glory.

Find joy in what Charles E. Jefferson said: "The principles of Jesus do not enthrone themselves in human society without the assistance of the church. The church is in literal truth the body of Jesus. Without it he does no mighty deeds. The amount of work which he accomplishes in every country is conditioned on the character of the church in that country. The kind of service he performs in any community is determined by the character of the Christian society in that community. Whenever the church prospers, society improves. Whenever the church languishes, society degenerates. When the church is vigorous and spiritual, the social atmosphere becomes bracing and clear; when the church becomes worldly and corrupt, the sun is turned into darkness and the moon into blood. The principles of Jesus take root in pagan lands only when they are planted there and watered by the church. The gospel would never have gotten out of Palestine had it not been for the Christian brotherhood, nor out of Europe into England had it not been for the church, nor out of the Old World into the New had the church not sent it. There is no hope for the triumph of the Christian religion outside the church. The church is not obsolescent. Humanity has not outgrown it. The noon is not behind it. Its triumphal career has only begun. We are toiling amid the mists of the early morning. It is the rising sun which smites our foreheads, and we cannot even dream of the glory which is to be. We work upon an enduring institution. After the flags of republics and empires have been blown to tatters, and the earth itself has tasted death, the church of Jesus shall stand forth glorious, free from blemish and mark of decay, the gates of Hades shall not prevail against it. Therefore, my beloved brethren, in these confused and confusing days, be steadfast, immovable in the presence of the world's clamor and rancor, always building your life and the lives of as many as God intrusts to your keeping, into the church of the Lord, forasmuch as you know that such labor is not in vain in the Lord."

Think upon what another says: "Persecution has not crushed the church; power has not beaten it back; time has not abated its force; the abuses and treasons of its friends have not shaken its stability."

Hark ye to this testimony from Spurgeon: "The church may go through her dark ages, but Christ is with her in the midnight. She may pass through her fiery furnace, but Christ is in the midst of the flames with her."

If we—and I speak particularly just now *to* and *of* Southern Baptists—would enlarge the place of our tent, there must be crucifixion with Christ. Where shall we find the moral and spiritual resources to make us effective in our "widened reach and heightened power"? They will be found where they have always been found —with Jesus. "They came to Jesus." These words point us to the conversion of the wild man of Gadara. When he was converted, the people of the near-by town "went out to see what it was that was done." And— "they came to Jesus."

Go out to see what has been done for the betterment of humanity—and you will come at the end to Jesus. Go out to see what has been done in hospitals—and you come to Jesus. Go out to see what has been done in orphanages —and you come to Jesus. Go out to see what has been done in social settlements—and you come to Jesus. Go out to see what has been done in homes for the needy—and you come to Jesus. Go out to see what has been done in multitudinous beneficent institutions, at home and abroad—and you come to Jesus. Go out to see who initiates prison reform, and you come to John Howard and Elizabeth Fry—and behind those devoted Christians you come to Jesus. Go out to see who began care for the insane—and you come to William Tuke, the Quaker, with the spirit of Christ. Go out to see who began work for underprivileged and neglected childhood—and you come to Lord Shaftsbury, a true Christian gentleman. Go out to see where indignation at the degradation of slum dwellings owes its beginnings—and you come to William Booth, the founder of the Salvation Army, a man who was dominated by Christ.

We must be able to say, individually: "I am crucified with Christ." And consecration is often the result of crucifixion, even as crucifixion is another name for consecration. I read this the other day: "When the Church is threatened with apostasy, endangered, corrupted, and degraded, there is no hope for it through painless preaching, painless living. It lives only as there are men who are willing to pour their lives out in the Church and for the Church. The blood of the martyrs is the seed of the Church. No redemption is possible without suffering."

And this: "The great redemptive power in life is the power of a suffering heart. No church can be lifted up into a higher plane except by a prophet who feels in his soul the pain, shame, and humiliation of all that is false and evil in the Church. No child was ever saved by an unsuffering mother, no nation by unsuffering patriots; no church by an unsuffering pastor; and—we say it reverently—the world could not be saved by an unsuffering God. He might take off the penalty; He might let us off; but He cannot pour His own life into us, so as to make us in very truth sons of God, unless He pours Himself into us through a wounded, riven, and broken heart."

And, from Lyman Abbott, this: "The angel who redeems Peter must go into the prison, that he may lead Peter out. The crucifixion was not an accident, an incident, an occasion. It was not something artificial, wrought by God for an artificial end. It was, in the very nature of the case, that the race could not be saved by a Redeemer who did not go down into the race, share its experiences, know its life, feel pressed by the burden of its degradation."

From the pen of Pastor G. C. Faulkner of Union, Missouri, come, with flames of fire, these words: "The cause of Jesus Christ is suffering defeat at home and abroad because Baptists will not die."

Have we not yet learned that the secret of daily living is daily dying? Do we believe that redeemed men are the harvest of the suffering and death of Jesus—not of his teaching and example? Know we yet that no work can ever be glorious without the martyr spirit? Do we believe that when luxury is a death blight upon our churches, the only remedy for it is the red blood of sacrifice? Are we willing to endure hardness as good soldiers of Jesus Christ? Are we courageous enough to be indifferent to popularity and human praise and human blame? Are we willing to live with great simplicity and most rigid economy? Are we Christlike enough to be willing to be misunderstood and persecuted? Are we wise enough to be the companions of the lowliest and the utterly despised? Are we able gladly to face toil and hardship and even death, and to count all things but loss for Christ and his kingdom? Shall we be guilty of the folly of being soldiers for splendid pageant and dress parade?

Jesus said: "If any man serve me, let him follow me." Is not what he actually means here that the only service he really recognizes is the Calvary kind? Is it not now and eternally true that the service which costs nothing counts for nothing? Is it not true, moreover, that service which costs will be abundantly and eternally rewarded? Somebody asks, "What is the law of the cross?" And the answer is that the cross is the gateway to glory, the path of life, the gauge of all service.

If we would make real in our lives and in the life of the world the figure of the enlarged tent and lengthened cords and strengthened stakes, there must be on our part compassionate concern. Frederick Taylor said: "It seems to me we have lost out of our Christian vocabulary the word 'concern'." But we must so live and so follow the example of Christ in seeking the lost that no man, in festering back alley or on the glittering boulevard—no woman in lazaretto or cafe—can say: "No man cared for my soul." With a wholesome irrepressibleness we must, here and there, in play and at work, at home and away from home, in church buildings and out of church buildings, lay on the hearts of men and women, young and old, and upon the hearts of boys and girls the claims of the Christ for their faith and service.

Let me ask some questions just here. Can Christ be a reality to us if we do not keenly feel that he is a necessity for others? Can we claim to get along *with* Christ so long as we feel that the world can get along *without* Christ? Can we make the world believe that we love him when we have no compassionate concern for those for whom he died? The mission of our churches is the mandate of the Master: "Go ye into all the world, and preach the gospel to every creature." The church that believes not this truth and practices not this truth is already negotiating for an inglorious grave.

'Tis tragically true, I fear, that when the great need of the hour is a holy passion for the souls of men, too many Christians keep a cold bath for every fervor. At a time when our churches should be distinguished by some clear and definite loyalties, is there not, on occasions, the policy of appeasement instead of the refusal to make any concession to evil?

On Whitefield's cenotaph is carved a flaming heart. Is it not true that, when it comes to Christly and compassionate concern for the lost, an icicle would be a more appropriate symbol for many hearts? Will we ever learn that a fool on fire is safer than a wise man on ice? Will we ever live and love as though we knew that conflagration and not refrigeration is our need?—that a high temperature in the service of Christ is better than a low pulse? Do we believe that coldness is death in the spiritual world as in the natural world? "Jesus wept." Shall we who profess to follow in Christ's train go our dry-eyed way, having handkerchiefs fragrant with perfume but never wet with tears of an anguished concern? Shall we remain unimpassioned by the love of God, having little or no agony of heart, manifesting little concern and little spiritual passion for eternity-marked souls? Shall we continue to spend no sleepless nights, no prayerful nights, on account of the precarious condition of those "without Christ and without hope" in this world? Shall we not the rather be out of breath pursuing souls? Shall we not the rather say to lost men and women what Whitefield once said: "I am willing to go to prison and to death *for* you, but I am not willing to go to heaven *without* you"?

Finally, to make real in our lives, in our homes, in our churches, in the world the glorious exhortations and imperatives of our text, we must here have the help of the Comforter. That great Comforter is the Holy Spirit. Jesus said: "But the Comforter, which is the Holy Ghost, whom the Father will send in my name, he shall teach you all things, and bring all things to your remembrance, whatsoever I have said unto you" (John 14:26).

Jesus said again: "Nevertheless I tell you the truth; it is expedient for you that I go away: for if I go not away, the Comforter will not come unto you; but if I depart, I will send him unto you" (John 16:7).

And again, note what Jesus said: "I have yet many things to say unto you, but ye cannot bear them now. Howbeit when he, the Spirit of truth, is come, he will guide you into all truth: for he shall not speak of himself; but whatsoever he shall hear, that shall he speak: and he will shew you things to come. He shall glorify me: for he shall receive of mine, and shall shew it unto you. All things that the Father hath are mine: therefore said I, that he shall take of mine, and shall shew it unto you" (John 16:12-15).

The Holy Spirit is the agent in the one great business of the church—making disciples of all nations, baptizing them, teaching them to observe the "all things" of

Christ's command. The Holy Spirit is the executive of the Godhead in all the work of God from creation to the end of all things. With the help of the Holy Spirit, we go forth conquering and to conquer. Without his cooperation, we shall be as a locomotive without steam, as an airplane without gasoline, as painted fire to warm a cold world, as painted bread to feed a hungry world. With him we shall not be victims of dawdling ditties but organs whose full breath is thunder—ourselves the keys beneath his fingers pressed—never, in our efforts, as an orchestra making mournful monotony of jangling inharmony.

Watkinson said: "Give that despairing musician an atom of Mozart's melodious brain—and music will swell from his instruments like thunder from the waves of the sea or whispers from summer zephyrs. Give that music master a bit of Beethoven's power—and surging seas of tone will be subservient to his rod. Give that bothered sculptor a slight measure of Angelo's skill and he will raise children unto God from the sterile womb of stone. Give that halting poet a spark of Shakespeare's fire—and verses will drop from his pen like golden pollen from the stems of shaken lilies. Give that struggling painter a nerve of Turner's color sense—and his brush will catch the waves and the winds and the mountains in it and that brush will spread crude paint into wondrous landscapes. Give that stammering tongue a lick of Demosthenes' tongue—and people will listen like frightened children to the roar of a storm or like slaves to an emancipation proclamation. Give that baffled scientist a bit of the investigative skill of Newton or Faraday—and the mysteries that confront will be made as simple as the alphabet to a scholar.'"[1]

In remembering Watkinson's beautiful words, let us do the greater thing of giving our bodies, our minds, our personalities, our talents, to the use of the Holy Spirit, and we shall make corner and continent conquests pleasing unto God.

In Ezekiel's day, the Spirit of God set Ezekiel down "in the midst of the valley which was full of dry bones"—bones that were very dry. That valley was a graveyard turned upside down; the ghastly, disjointed bones scattered over all parts. Scavengers had done their work—sinews gone!—flesh gone!—skin gone! But as Ezekiel, by the command of God, prophesied, "there was a noise, and behold a shaking, and the bone came together, bone to his bone."

"Noise" "shaking"—"coming together"—"getting together." Fleshless skulls, grinning hideously, rolling in that valley with noise of wooden balls, striking tenpins in a bowling alley. Shoulder blades scuffling over other bones with the noise of shutters rattling in a storm. Ribs, like baskets of gravel pouring down and out tin pipes. Kneecaps, with the noise of huge dice thrown about in tin tubs, scattering here and there. Bones of toes and fingers, a scrawling mass of disjointed ivory, assembling themselves. Thigh bones with the noise of dry cedar tops whipped by a cyclone, like rough boards rubbed on sandpaper, came to the formation of the body long decayed—in promiscuous ditches. Pigmy bodies and giant bodies—of bones, then sinews, flesh, skin—

[1]Watkinson, *The Bane and the Antidote* (New York: Fleming H. Revell Company) p. 181.

BODIES. Then as Ezekiel looked upon that scene, "the sinews and the flesh came upon them, and the skin covered them above." BUT—"there was no breath in them."

The bone yard had changed to a morgue. The organized bones were as impotent as a gun in a dead man's hands—as impotent as when they lay scattered over the desolate fields. "Noise." "Shaking." "Coming together." "Getting together." Yes. But no enlivening power from the heart of God. Noise, shaking, coming together. But no inspiration, no aspiration, no pervading breath, no sacrifice, no shedding of blood. Just an organized corpse!

"Then he said unto me, Prophesy unto the wind, prophesy, son of man, and say to the wind, Thus saith the Lord God; come from the four winds, O breath, and breathe upon these slain, that they may live" (Ezekiel 37:9). Then there was the flutter of ten thousand eye lids. Then there was the flash of life light in ten thousand eyes. Then there was the flush of blood in ten thousand cheeks. Then there was the beating of ten thousand hearts. Then there was the breathing of ten thousand lungs. Then there was the moving of ten thousand hands. Then there was the listening of ten thousand ears. Then there was the speech of ten thousand lips and tongues. Then there was the bending of ten thousands of knees. Then there was the manipulation of one hundred thousand fingers. Then there was the suppleness of millions of miles of muscles. Then there was the pumping of millions of gallons of blood through veins and arteries. Then there were ten thousand shoulders ready for burdens. Then there were ten thousand arms ready for embracing or thrusting away. Then there were ten thousand bodies ready for clothing. Gone the bone yard. Gone the morgue. There they stood—many, many bodies—thus described: "And the breath came into them, and they lived, and stood up upon their feet, an exceeding great army" (Ezekiel 37:10). "Not by might nor by power, but by my Spirit, saith the Lord."

Come, O Breath! Be this the hour!
Come, O Breath of God, with power,
Ere the depths of hell devour
Those who sleep in sin!

Come, O Breath! Thy might we crave!
Hear our cry! Make haste to save!
Speak and call them from their grave!
Bid new life begin.

To which we make plea. Come, O Spirit of God, from behind the threatening clouds of race prejudice and make them to clasp hands in friendship. Come from beyond the chasms across which men glare at one another in suspicion and ill-will and enable them to love their neighbors as themselves. Come into the midst of scientific wonders lest science continue to be the perverted apostle of savagery. Come into the midst of university and college and seminary and high school life and manifest thy power so that there shall not be that intellectual conceit unaware of the rattle of its dry bones—so that we shall not be guilty of possessing a superficial mental illumination that lacks the urge of sacrificial passion. Come into the midst of the parliaments of men—where Christ is ignored or patronized—and breathe upon them that they may believe that Christ is the only hope for our head-dizzy, war-wounded, heartbroken, soul-famished world.

Come, O Breath of God, and breathe upon the nations which now wear the funeral wreath upon their brow that they may come forth to the life that will glorify thee in acknowledgment of thy greatness and goodness—glorify thee in obedience to thy law.

Come, O Breath, and breathe upon our slain hopes and cold worship and loveless marital relationships and bone yards of thought and morgues void of spiritual vitality that they may live. Then shall we be "more than conquerors through Christ who loved us." Amen.

Note.—Delivered before the Southern Baptist Convention, noon, Saturday, May 18, 1946, Miami, Florida.

III

The Missionary Challenge of the New South

A sense of woeful inadequacy oppresses me as I come to this hour. I am glad to speak for Jesus, but I fear I shall fall far short. I fear that I would appear as one who waters the lawn during a cloudburst if I should talk to you of "churning the milk of the country churches"; of planting missions in cities; of "Christianizing the pagan foreigners" among us lest they paganize us; of the danger of losing Baptist leadership of the Negro race while their danger is following red-eyed radicals rather than spiritually religious leadership. If such were the content of this address, I would say what Anthony said at Caesar's funeral: "I only speak right on; I tell you that which you yourselves do know," even as I can say what, later, Octavia said to Anthony:

> For we are at stake,
> And bay'd about with many enemies;
> And some that smile have in their hearts, I fear,
> Millions of mischiefs.

Yet if this message prevents the tragedy of some church or individual "being armed and carrying bows, turning back in the day of battle,'' I shall gladly suffer the humiliation of failure and consequent criticism—at a time when there are the increasing purgations of war and Hitler thrusting the rapiers of his panzer divisions into the breasts of nations. ''The Missionary Challenge of the New South!''

I. The New South

It is new. Yet old. Flowers, fringed with God's glory, jonquil gold, magnolia snow, roses setting their frail jars of perfume everywhere—are the same as when first slept ''under the roses the Blue, and under the lilies the Gray.'' Rivers murmur as of old. Same mountains sentinel the same sweet valleys. The same old fields, at the call of the cotton gin, spread their white garments.

The same old hills with aromatic pines. The same old sun, with golden fingers, embroiders the meadows with flowers. The same old moon blossoms like a huge jonquil in God's star gardens. Mockingbirds, the Beethoven of the boughs, sing as in the dear, dead days beyond recall. With us still the black race—as black as when Negro troops facing British bullets in the battle of New Orleans won the praise of General Jackson—with songs as weirdly sweet as when Negro mammies sang lullabies to white children in their ebony arms. Death, whose only pleasure fountains are the falling tears, is with us. And sin, forever blasting all that is fair, is the same. Satan who, in Eden, slandered God to man—who, in Job's day, slandered man to God, is still here; and slavery, though human bodies are no longer property in human flesh, is here, for men are in bondage to evils more cruel than Simon Legree's whip. Old is the South as to contour, as to love, heartaches, beautiful women and foolish women, gallant men and villainous men. But the Old South, a queenly beauty, imperious and exacting, with the North, an obsequious suitor, kneeling at her feet while both parties, Whig and Democrat, drank of the cup of her sorcery, is "gone with the wind."

From the Old South we received the crude plow, the scythe, the ferry; we bequeath the tractor, the mowing machine, the ocean greyhound. We received the beacon signal fire, the tallow candle, the bellows; we bequeath wireless telegraphy, the incandescent light, the blast furnace. We received the little red schoolhouse; we bequeath consolidated schools. We received the kite, the buggy, the covered wagon with a calendar for a timetable; we bequeath the airplane, the automobile, the locomotive, massive juggernaut of steel and steam. We received the old rail fence which wormed its way like a huge weather-beaten serpent too old to crawl; we bequeath the far-reaching barbed wire fence shining like a huge spider web. We received the old milk jar and barn lantern; we bequeath the cream separator and the flashlight. We received spades, stairways, treadmills; we bequeath steam shovels, escalators, hydraulic elevators, which make our modern skyscrapers possible. We received the flintlock musket; we bequeath machine guns and cannon that shoot two thousand pounds twenty miles. We received the sledge hammers; we bequeath the pile driver. We received washpots and clotheslines; we bequeath steam laundries. We received diphtheria; we bequeath the antitoxin which makes it so that the black wings of that dread disease flutter but seldom over any cradle. We received yellow fever; we bequeath the sanitary marvel that makes it so that no more do people evacuate cities in vain attempt to escape death that once made invasion—riding the thin, gauzy wings of the mosquito. We received the almanac; we bequeath the radio weather reports. We received only dirt roads; we bequeath the hard-surfaced roads, like the benevolent octopus arms, running to all sections. We received blacksmith shops, livery stables, hitching posts; we bequeath garages, parking lots, parking meters. We received sectional passion—South fighting North at Chancellorsville, Cold Harbor, Gettysburg; we bequeath an aggressive patriotism—the South and the North dying at Pearl Harbor, battling on Bataan, struggling in farflung battle lines, determined to make secure the imperiled liberties of our land. Once the South was free from all sorts of foreign innovations and alien customs; there were few who did not implicitly believe the Bible. Now we find some riding in the fantastic yacht of "Advanced Thought" (God protect us!) which leaks at the prow, leaks at the stern, and has a steel pen for one oar and a glib tongue for the other oar.

I walk not with the presumptuous step of a know-it-all. I drive no garbage cart when I say that our Home Mission Board never faced such a dark world or homeland. Today, nations have tobogganed into chaos. The human race is bankrupt. Monarchy, republicanism, dictatorship, democracy have failed. Daring defiances by supercilious poses, by attitudes of intellectual superiority, by skeptical attitudes toward the supernatural, substitute man-made philosophies and pseudo-science for the living Word of God's revelation—parroting the skepticism of free thinkers. While Mars walks with bloody boots, tying crepe to millions of doorknobs, unreasonable devotions to sensual satisfactions and mad scrambles after gain abound. An undisciplined liberalism goes nowhere so fast it arrives out of breath. The Bible is summoned to appear at the bar of human reason. Spiritual mercury falls low. Black snow falls. Faith's wings are clipped by reason's scissors. There is the administration of laughing gas for the painless extraction of sin. Philistines of transcendent cleverness submit the warm wonder of Christianity to cool and merciless analysis. Fat deformities ask us to substitute for Christianity's vital bread a chunk of cloud bank buttered with the night wind. This day of invertebrate theology, jellyfish morality, India-rubber convictions, seesaw religion, somersault philosophy, and spiritual latitudes wide as the Sahara Desert and as correspondingly dry—finds civilization undergoing the frightful processes of self-burial. For the corruptions of Moloch, the spirit of unjust power, and Belial, the spirit of unholy pleasure, and Mammon, the spirit of unrighteous gain, inhabit our frail blood. There is the tendency to idolize science, so that thousands of people undertake to interpret everything in terms of natural phenomena, reducing the supernatural to ignorance. Amid bloody struggles for military supremacy Christianity is reduced to the status of humanism, social service, national therapy—with the resulting tendency to undermine faith and destroy the passion for souls.

Describing our day more than, as some believe, his day, Victor Hugo said:

> . . . In this boasted march of wrong and error,
> 'Mid the vast splendor of an age that glows,

One thing, O Jesus, fills my heart with terror:
The echo of Thy voice still feebler grows!

Nero, fiddling while Rome burned, was a playful eccentric compared with tyrants and dictators now torturing the world. Today, while a collective insanity, a laughless imbecility, hurls humanity into the pit of destruction, millions of martyred believers make us know that the persecution of Christians under Nero was small in comparison with the wholesale slaughter of Christ's disciples now. Government of the people, by the people, for the people has perished from this universe of debauchery, mediocrity, chicanery, collapse—while, "as fishes taken in an evil net, as birds caught in a snare, so are the sons of men snared in an evil time." What shall the watchman on the towers say to people in this hate-blackened world, loosing wild tongues, shaking defiant fists, definitely antagonistic to God, lying in the power of the evil one?

II. Our Missionary Challenge

A challenge, meaning "a calling in question," involves a challenger.

Who dares this pair of boots displace,
Must meet Bombastes face to face;
Thus do I challenge all the human race.

Today, evils that would lead our greatest graces to the grave and leave the world no copy challenge the superiority of Christian truth with all the bombastic strength and arrogance of Goliath of Gath. Infidelity and atheism challenge Christianity—pouring anathemas upon it. Philosophies call in question all we believe and teach. The fury of life's fierce heat burns divine dew off the grass. As in law, there is the "Challenge of the Array," i.e., an objection to the whole panel or body of jurymen. So in life today are "isms" and evils that challenge us to prove the superiority of what we believe.

Serving Christ brings us at once into conflict with all forces arrayed against him. In the midst of a world which not only declares "we will not have this man to reign over us," but is ever alert to hinder the progress of Christ's churches, darkness and light, summer and winter, liberty and bondage, cannot both have ultimate triumph.

In Palestine two opposing civilizations came into collision—one was the Hebrew and the other the Philistine; and the Philistine went down. In Holland the Dutchman, working toward democracy, collided with the Spaniards, working toward autocracy; and the Spaniards went down. In England, Hampden and Pym came into collision with Charles I and Archbishop Laud. The two leaders of democracy wished the increase of the privileges of the common people by diffusing property, liberty, office, and honor, while Charles I and Laud wished to lessen the powers of the people and to increase the privileges of the throne; democracy won, autocracy lost.

In the New South, two forces are arrayed against each other—chilling, killing formalism and evangelism. For them to join hands and hearts for the good of humanity is like expecting Isaac, the son of the free woman, and Ishmael, the son of the slave woman, to be affectionate under the same roof.

Once the North Pole challenged men. It said to all races of men: Come on, I'll starve you with my barren wastes. Come on, I'll stab you with my frosty daggers.

Come on, I'll crush your iron ships with my continental ice. Come on, I'll freeze you and sing your funeral hymn with my blizzardly winds. Come on, I'll cover your grave with my blankets of snow. Be it said to the glory of the American race, the challenge was answered, and man breathed his victorious exclamations and unfurled our flag at the North Pole. More victoriously may we meet every challenge of all foes, with faith in God who gave David victory over Goliath of Gath. May every word we speak be like Lyman Beecher said about Webster's reply to Hayne: "His speech reminds me of a red hot cannon ball going through a pile of egg shells."

III. What Must Be Done to Answer the Challenge Aright?

1. We must *Reach the Unreached*

There are twenty-five million unsaved in the Southland—multitudes to whom the gospel means nothing. Four thousand, seven hundred and sixty people die, on an average, every hour. Only one hundred and fifty-four out of that number are professing Christians. Unreached in mountain lands, villages, towns, country places, cities—multitudes misled and unled. The unchurched multitudes are a challenge to our integrity and life. The forces of evil do not sleep; they seek to destroy. They clothe themselves in attractive garments. They use subtle means to accomplish their evil designs. Hesitant churches cannot defeat them.

The parables of the ninety and nine, the lost coin, the pearl of great price, our Lord's experience with Zaccheus, his conversation with the rich young ruler, his tears for unrepented Jerusalem—all these and other teachings and the example of our Lord rise up to rebuke us if we dare leave anyone beyond the range of our effort. To all these multitudes we must give thought and heart. Like Jesus, when he saw the multitudes, we must be *moved* with compassion, not simply *touched* with compassion, not the surface of his nature rippled. He was stirred through and through. His whole inner life was shaken—swept as by a storm. As he was moved with anger amid the seclusions of fraud in the temple, so he was moved with compassion, seeing the people as shepherdless, silly sheep—missing the road. When he drew nigh the city, he wept over it. Crowds cheering! Throngs strewing flowers! But above their hosannas the sobs of Christ! Jerusalem, "beautiful for situation," the joy of the whole earth! The temple—forty and six years in building! Palace for king! Palace for high priest! Playgrounds! Pageants! Grand Theater! Hippodrome! Three historic towers! An acropolis! But these caught not the eyes of Jesus! The Lord of glory weeping, because multitudes knew not the things that belonged to their peace.

Such multitudes are here now. We must go after them in the spirit of our Saviour who came to seek and to save that which was lost and who bade us to go into the highways and the hedges and bring the people in. We need to pray God to give us compassionate hearts for the unsaved all about us. With the passion of these who have glimpsed the Shekinah in the holy place, in the spirit of him who wept over Jerusalem, we must translate from the desire to the deed the words:

> I thirst, I faint, I die to prove
> The greatness of redeeming love.

And thou, Solomon, my son, know thou the God of thy father, and serve him with a perfect heart and with a willing mind: for the Lord searcheth all hearts, and understandeth all the imaginations of the thoughts: if thou seek him, he will be found of thee; but if thou forsake him, he will cast thee off forever (1 Chronicles 28:9).

Not with a perfect *head* but with a perfect *heart.* Our heads will not be perfect in *wisdom,* but our hearts may be perfect in *love.* Our heads may betray us into errors of judgment, but when our hearts are perfect in *love,* our service is acceptable unto God.

Once my little daughter, when her mother was away, was keeping house. I came in and asked if she could get supper for me. She very happily consented, and ran to the kitchen. She lit the gas stove. Soon I smelled the odor of frying meat. Soon the house was full of grease smoke. The rattle of dishes was ominous. Soon I smelled burned bread. I heard a plate fall and break. When at last she called me to the table, the biscuits were heavy and burned. The meat was first cousin to a cinder. One dish had a bit of soap on it. Her face was flushed. Her finger had a blister. The service was *imperfect,* but the *love* was perfect! She was doing my will from the heart.

Paul says: "Doing the will of God from the heart." As the blacksmith puts his strength into the stroke, as the bee puts its life into its sting, so let us put heart into the struggle. When the heart grows cold, the principle of growth ceases, spiritual vision waxes faint and unsure, the spontaneity of obedience ceases, inspiration of sacrifice is wanting, boast of orthodoxy becomes vain, the magic of virtue is no more. A truly Christian life cannot be maintained on cold calculation, mere intellectual assent, ecclesiastical routine and ceremony.

A book was published in England entitled *Modern Christianity a Civilized Heathenism.* The gist of this book is how far we have fallen from Christ's earnestness. The author holds that the chief note of Christ's character and teaching is its all-consuming fervor, while the chief note of his followers is their general lukewarmness and lethargy. The climax of the book is that if Jesus lived today, the church would put him in an asylum. This is a startling indictment. Is it true? What of ourselves? If the Lord of glory came among us today, would we receive him? He was warm; we, cold. He was enthusiastic; we, indifferent. His fire was real; ours, painted. He wept over Jerusalem; we rarely weep over any city. Has there been a cooling down of the church's temperature? Has the thermometer dropped? Are we prosaic? Are we lethargic? Have we lost the fine flavor of our early rapture? Are we strangely afraid of demonstration? Are our eyes aglow? Do our hearts burn? Do we, like Joseph, interpret to people their dreams—drive gaunt famine from their doors by the penetration of our judgments and the foresight of our vision? Do we go ahead of a timid diplomacy, spying out lands which the worldly wise have declared unconquerable, and, returning, bear grapes of Eschol in our hands, rebuking people's despondency by the courage of our faith and curing their faintheartedness by the hopefulness of our lives?

2. We must *Dig Up the Dormant in Our Churches*

Too many churches are rest camps, playgrounds, ecclesiastical nurseries. Too many, needing iron in the blood, sick with spiritual diabetes—too much sugar—are church enemies through utter apathy—described in Job: "The oxen were plowing and the asses feeding beside them." More troublesome than ever were the Midianites to Israel are the lazyites who are as poor soldiers as gouty men trying to walk—entrenched behind walls of sheer indifference. What a missionary challenge to our churches with so many do-nothings, do-littles, and don't-cares. If an auto had as many useless parts as the average church, it would not run downhill. If an airplane had as many nonfunctioning parts as the average church, it would fly no higher and go no further than a canary bird with a sack of wheat tied to its tail. If as many letters seceded from the alphabet as we have men who withhold themselves from service in the church, what consternation in every print shop! If as many stars dropped from the sky as we have members who have dropped out for no commendable cause, astronomical adversities would beset our world.

Does not history prove that the continuance of Christianity is dependent on the church? Do the principles of Jesus enthrone themselves in human society without the assistance of the church? No. Whenever the church prospers, society improves. Whenever the church languishes, society degenerates. When the church is vigorous and spiritual, the social atmosphere becomes bracing and clear; when the church becomes worldly and corrupt, the sun is turned into darkness and the moon into blood. The principles of Jesus take root in pagan lands only when they are planted there and watered by the church. There is no hope for the triumph of the Christian religion outside the church. After the flags of republics and empires have been blown to tatters and the earth itself has tasted death, the church of Jesus shall stand forth gloriously free from blemish and mark of decay; the gates of Hades shall not prevail against it. Therefore, my beloved brethren, in these confused and confusing days, be steadfast, unmovable in the presence of the world's clamor and rancor, always building your life and the lives of as many as God entrusts to your keeping, into the church of the Lord, forasmuch as you know that such labor is not in vain in the Lord.

Among the words of Joseph Parker in his last sermon in the City Temple are these: "As long as the church of God is one of many institutions she will have her little day. She will die, and that will be all; but just as soon as she gets the spirit of Jesus Christ, until the world thinks she had gone stark mad, then we shall be on the highroad to capturing this planet for Jesus Christ."

3. We must *Glorify God by the Sacrifice of Selfishness*

In the most remarkable prayer ever prayed, Jesus said: "I have glorified thee on the earth." How we would remove mountains and quit rolling marbles, make conquest of continents rather than corners, rid our land of self-satisfied religious mediocrity, change the foulness of Rome into the fragrance of New Jerusalem, save churches from becoming "drifting sepulchres manned by frozen crews," if preachers, if presidents of institutions, if editors, if teachers, if deacons, if Sunday school officers, if businessmen—all of us—would glorify God by the sacrifice of selfishness. Christianity makes one generic requirement—the sacrifice of selfishness. Sacrifice here means destruction. Selfishness, the principle which prompts man to seek the promotion of his own supposed interest in disregard of the will of God, the insanity of existence, the apostasy of being, must be slain. This is the all-comprehensive demand of Christianity. It is idle to collect facts or compose arguments here. Selfishness, the very soul of sin, opposed to the example of Christ, must be put out of sight.

In the New South with the oil of war, black and sulphureous, we are anointed for high priest services in heroism. Our insulted flag, millions of men in arms, garments rolled in blood, ghastly heaps of dead men on desperate battlefields, thousands gasping their last amid blood bubbles of submarine-endangered and shark-infested waters, the inevitably enlarging army of slowly moving cripples, and graveyards becoming as populous as cities, make us to know we cannot smell blood of battlefields as though it were perfume from quiet gardens—remaining unmoved.

4. Wisely to meet this challenge, we must *Re-enact Calvary*

I do not say that any man or set of men can atone for sin, or that our cross can be a substitute for Christ's cross. But if Christ's cross is real to us, it must be an experience, not merely a memory. We must not merely sing but make real in our lives the hymn which has within it the words:

> My richest gain I count but loss,
> And pour contempt on all my pride.

We must not look on one night's toothache as a year of sciatica agonies, not be victims of an easy track, not anchor in our snug little Galilee when the oceans roll. We must not. The mightiest men of all the ages have been mightiest in their agonies. And to them the cross meant more than a lovely song handed over to the lips of expert singers. The cross must mean more than an architectural splendor, more than a pretty way of ending a spire, more than a piece of jewelry dangling from a man's watch chain or from a woman's neck. All the anxieties, tears, and griefs of humanity are to be taken in the reckoning. In suffering, everything must be claimed for him, everything sealed with the King's seal, every talent used for his exclusive glory. We cannot know the fellowship of his suffering if we choose ease, if we prefer the protected areas of life, if we seek safety beyond the battle lines or get the fighting spirit when the battle is over. Our service must not stop when the blood letting begins.

Shall the spirit of Abraham be in us? He, in obedience and by faith, "went out, not knowing whither he went," looking for "a city which hath foundations, whose builder and maker is God." Shall the spirit of Moses? He "chose to suffer affliction with the people of God." Shall the spirit of Elijah? He, God's prophet of fire in an apostate age, grieved only when God's cause seemed to totter. Shall the spirit of Samuel? He called the people back to the faith of their fathers, rekindling the flame of high religious life, though he himself was discarded and disparaged. Shall the spirit of Joseph? He went to jail for righteousness' sake! Shall the spirit of Ezekiel? Suffering, he was the chaplain marching with a nation condemned to the execution place—preaching individual responsibility, hearing amid the wailings of captivity the whir of angel's wings. Shall the spirit of Baruch? In the age of disloyalty, he was loyal. Born to wealth and the life of a prince, he was happy to be friend, amanuensis to Jeremiah. Shall the spirit of John the Baptist? Descending upon the iniquities of his day with a torch in one hand and a sword in the other, he said of Jesus, "He must increase, but I must decrease." Shall the spirit of Paul? Until he met Jesus, his life was a mournful monotony of jangling inharmony, missing life's central melody, because he was a victim of dawdling ditties. After that his life was a thrilling one of hardship, hazards, heroism. Shall the spirit of Christ? He set his face down the road blocked yonder by a bloody cross—and would not be turned aside. Shall the spirit of Luther be in us? At a time when civilization was bruising her wings against iron-barbed despotisms, he "folded his passions like a tent" to take his place in the armies of God. Shall the spirit of Job be in us? Voicing the anguish of generations, asking God questions through lips festering with disease, standing in the dark pleading for light, he said: "Though he slay me, yet will I trust in him." Shall the spirit of Amos be in us? At a time when the scepter was frozen with the tyranny of impeached civilizations, he summoned nations to judgment, urging men to prepare to meet God. If the spirit of these men be ours, then shall we make the spiritual supreme in the New South, indeed!

History teaches that material forces can never win moral and spiritual victories. If we assume that they can, we fly in the face of the teachings of history. Down a thousand roads are we ignoring that teaching?

"O World-God, give me wealth!" the Egyptian cried.
His prayer was granted. High as heaven, behold
Palace and pyramid; the brimming tide
Of lavish Nile washed all his land with gold.

Armies of slaves toiled ant-wise at his feet,
World-circling traffic roared through mart and street,
His priests were gods, his spice-balmed kings enshrined,
Set death at naught in rock-ribbed channels deep.
Seek Pharaoh's race today and ye shall find,
Rust and the moth, silence and dusty sleep.

"O World-God, give me beauty!" cried the Greek.
His prayer was granted. All the earth became
Plastic and vocal to his sense; each peak,
Each grove, each stream, quick with Promethean flame,
Peopled the world with imaged grace and light.
The lyre was his, and his the breathing might
Of the immortal marble, his the play
Of diamond-pointed thought, and golden tongue.
Go seek the sunshine race. Ye find today
A broken column and a lute unstrung.

"O World-God, give me power!" the Roman cried.
His prayer was granted. The vast world was chained
A captive to the chariot of his pride.
The blood of myriad provinces was drained
To feed that fierce, insatiable red heart.
Invulnerably bulwarked every part
With serried legions and with close-meshed Code.
Within, the burrowing worm had gnawed its home.
A roofless ruin stands where once abode
The imperial race of everlasting Rome.[1]

5. To meet this missionary challenge, we must put forth *Heart-winning Preaching and Living*

Athenian society decayed, not because its artists had reached the limit of human invention or philosophers the necessary term of human thought, but because the moral faculties and tastes which should have been presented in that society were not developed in proportion to the

[1]Emma Lazarus, "Gifts" (Boston: Houghton-Mifflin Company.) Used by permission.

aesthetic and the intellectual. No victory is finally effective which does not capture the ramparts of the soul. We never win a man until the heart is won. If the heart be missed, the man escapes. This is taught on every page of history. Win the heart and you capture the life. It is so in friendship. It is so in marriage. It is so in the life of a people or race. Capture the heart and the citadel surrenders.

This is our crusade as world citizens. We are to win the hearts of humanity for Christ. We must capture the Irish heart, the Negro heart, the Hindoo heart, the German heart, the Russian heart—the heart of all races. Nothing else will suffice. Anything else will leave us tragically in arrears. Experience shouts this warning down a thousand different roads. History records this lesson on every page and in every chapter. And we ourselves are more fully emancipated when we seek another's freedom. We ourselves are warmed at the fire we kindle for another. Napoleon said: "I conquer provinces, Josephine wins hearts—and her's is the greater victory." John Paul Jones fought as though the whole cause of American liberty depended on him. We must preach as though the saving of all the lost and the welfare of all the churches depended on us. We cannot medicate volcanoes into quietude and stop sin's plague by administering political quinine. Moonlight ripens no harvest. But if the fire is in our hearts, the flame will be in our mouths. We cannot thaw man's wintry bondage with theatrical fire. Surely the sins and sorrows of our people must fall on our hearts—not as sparks on ice but as sparks on a prairie, quickly kindling into a conflagration. It was not polished, erudite Erasmus, but rough, red-hot

Martin Luther who made Germany. We have enemies of the gospel—battalions of iniquity—who cannot be conquered by rose water and soft speeches. Soft sermons in morocco cases, laid down in front of an exquisite audience, will not do it. Sending missives as delicate as wedding cards, asking the black giant of sin if he will surrender, will not. Riding white palfreys under embroidered housing, putting the spurs in just enough to make the charger dance gracefully, will not. Indignation against the Hittites and the Jebusites will not. Coveting no phraseology that lends respectability to sin, we must apply our indignation to modern transgressions which need to be hewn as Samuel hewed Agag. Jesus left us an example. Some of his sayings are sweet with consolations, some divinely catastrophic, creating, and destructive. They are all in a way completely new. Though preaching his sayings, we seem mad to the world, we must not hesitate to be as "wild-eyed mariners between whirlpools and waterspouts, their masts quivering and rocking as the ship tosses, but his bowsprit steadily pointing to the Southern Cross." This is not an hour for discouragement. The valley of trouble, in the providence of God, is always a door of hope. We must learn to be ruthless with ourselves. Discouragement, in both peace and war, may be due to the illusion that life was meant to be an easy thing.

Let me urge all men everywhere to

IV. Hold the Assurance That Jesus Will Finally Conquer and Truth Will Ultimately Prevail

This is the time to remember Revelation 17:14: These shall make war with the Lamb, and the Lamb shall overcome them: for he is Lord of lords, and King of kings: and they that are with him are called, and chosen, and faithful.

Jesus acknowledges no mastery in hostile circumstances. Centuries do not leave him behind. He offers the inexhaustible fountains of his strength. He keeps pace with the most unexpected challenges. He changes black limitation into immeasurable expanse. He enables us to become headwaters of benediction to others. When the Roman general, Pompey, was warned against the danger of his return from Egypt to Italy, he said: "It is a small matter that I go forward and die; it is too great a matter if I should take one step backward and live."

With the glorious Home Mission Board report still in our ears and warm in our hearts, shall we not renew our allegiance to Christ this night? Let it be known of us by those who come after us that the ark of the covenant, which has guided man from Egypt's darkness to Canaan's light, from paganism to civilization, from spiritual province to spiritual power, from superstition to Christianity, has been carried by the stainless hands of high priests of piety and intelligence who, watching and following God's pillar of cloud, led the people from the house of bondage into a land flowing with milk and honey. Let our children tell it to generations following that impassable seas knew us at our approach, and the obsequious waves, out of reverence for our work, parted at our coming, making a dry path for our passage and for the passing of the people who follow us. May our faith, our sacrifice, be such that it shall be said of us that swollen streams ceased to flow to let us go by, that walled cities fell down at the call of the stirring notes of our silver trumpets. Let us, under the push of the past, the pressure of the present, the lure of the future, be near enough to God "to be the gloves on the hand of his power," to be the keys beneath his fingers pressed on his organ whose full breath is thunder.

Sometimes after reading the pages of history and seeing how men and women paid allegiance to earthly kings and to human leaders, I think how poor is the allegiance we pay to Jesus Christ. You remember when Napoleon took his great army and marched to Russia? Four hundred thousand men started out on that great campaign, and only forty thousand bedraggled, starved, emaciated soldiers ever found their way back to Paris.

When he marched on Moscow, the Russians set fire to their city; and there was no alternative for Napoleon except to turn around and return to France. He went to Marshall Ney and said: "You are in charge of the rear guard. Keep the Russians back from my main army. Hold them back at any cost that I can get my men safely back with me to Paris." And Marshall Ney gathered his faithful troops around him and they fought their way back bit by bit. And the cold nights set in. These men loved their Marshall. He would lie down to sleep at night in a little improvised tent. One morning when he got up feeling warm, he found he had been covered with overcoats. When he stepped out of the door of his tent, there were two soldiers standing there stiff and erect on either side. They were frozen dead. They had not their overcoats on. And when they made improvised bridges, some of the men plunged into the icy cold waters and held up the parapets while the rear guard went over. As Marshall Ney went over, he pinned the cross of the Legion of

Honor of France on the breasts of the dead men as they stood frozen in the icy water.

One day, away back in Paris, there were four young officers playing cards, and there appeared in the door of the room, an old, dusty, bent man. His tunic was torn, his hair was matted over his face, he was covered with dust from head to foot. One of the young officers jumped to his feet and said: "It is Marshall Ney." The other three arose to salute. They said: "Marshall, tell us, where is the rear guard?" The old soldier squared his shoulders, and said: "Sirs, I am the rear guard." It was almost literally true, for he alone was left.

Tell me, if men will owe allegiance to a human leader like that, what is your allegiance worth to Jesus Christ? Are you standing with him in the conflict down here on earth? Will you hear again his call tonight, and from your heart say, "He is Lord of lords and King of kings?" Will you gladly arise and go to endure hardness as a good soldier of Jesus Christ?—standing in the battle line, declaring war against everything that dishonors the glory of Christ?

High resolve preluding holy venture! Review! Repentance! Then purpose, prayer, program! Yesterday's record is locked, and the key is in the hand of God. Crosses or coronations, tears or triumphs, joys or jolts, difficulties and dangers or delights, we are yet undaunted. Nations must enthrone the Prince of Peace to master the monster, militarism. The church of Christ must lift in love the Son of God and worship him as God the Son. Then shall meridian splendor be before us, not behind us. God reigns! Take heart!

Yes, take heart!—praying that God will cure us of our blindness that we may see past the tall buildings of our cities and see those wretched and miserable in sin and sorrow and shame.

Take heart!—and see past the dark material into and upon the luminous spiritual, keeping out of scientific and upon the fluid things eternal.

Take heart!—and see past the hard things visible into fog banks that make you see not Jesus only.

Have faith!—and see beyond greed to the luxury of giving.

Have faith!—and see past pride to the sunny healthfulness of humility, past the heart of desire to the light of renunciation, past the glare of power to the abiding beauty of service, past the rank and poisonous growth of self to the flower and fragrance of unself.

Have faith!—looking past worldliness to spirituality, past night to renewing dawn, past gloom to glory, past death to eternal life, past the finite to the infinite, past men and things and events to God—remembering ever, forgetting never, that "they that are with him are called and chosen and faithful."

NOTE.—Address given before the Southern Baptist Convention, 1942.

IV

The Constant Call of Christ's Cross

And when she had so said, she went her way, and called Mary her sister secretly, saying The Master is come, and calleth for thee.—John 11:28.

Mrs. Browning, the woman Shakespeare of England and of the world, taught that our ears and hearts are besieged and assaulted by calls. She said, "World-voices east, world-voices west."

We live in a world of calls.

There are bird calls—some as raucous as the crow's voice and some as sweet as the lyrics of the lark, the Mendelsohns of the meadows, and as melodious as the many-voiced mockingbird, the Beethoven of the boughs.

There are fire calls—with loud alarms, when fire, man's good servant, is master.

There are factory calls—with shrieking whistles that summon to work or rest.

There is the call of the wild—when men prefer the wolf's howl to human voices.

There are the calls to arms—to which men respond, willing to choose garments of flame and blood for garments of service.

There are political calls—when many fingers point many eyes to ballot boxes.

There are love calls—which were old when the Pyramids were new and which are as young as the flowers that blossomed this morning and as multitudinous as the stars.

There are calls of distress—as when the *Titantic* went down.

But I would ask you today to pitch your mental tent in the councils of eternity, in Egypt, in Palestine, at Calvary—and consider the call of Christ's cross.

It is

I. Call to Thought About the Preparation of the Cross

The cross, where the history of human guilt culminates, was conceived in the councils of eternity, where Father, Son, and Holy Ghost knew infinite rejoicing without interruption or diminution.

The cross, where the purposes of divine love are made intelligible, was made ready while Jesus had glory with God before the world was, while he was loved by the Father before the foundation of the world—for then the cross was conceived in the mind of God.

The cross, where the majesty of the law is vindicated,
where the problem of human redemption is
solved,

where the fountain of salvation is unsealed, was a reality in heaven before ever there was an earth.

The cross, where Satan is crushed,
where our sorrows hide in Emmanuel's wounds,
where our death sentence is revoked, was a goal in the heart of God from all eternity.

The cross was prepared in heaven before creation—and, amidst the angels of heaven who worshiped Christ. Jesus *felt* the weight of the cross ages before he *fell* beneath its weight in the midst of men who despised him and women who wept over him.

Though it is a tremendous subject and as far beyond and above our mental capacity to comprehend as a teaspoon lacks capacity to hold a ton of sand, still God would be pleased and we will be profited to give thought to the preparation of the cross.

Give thought to the majesty of it.
Give thought to the mystery of it.
Give thought to the eternity of it.
Give thought to the wisdom that conceived it.
Give thought to the love that prepared it.
Give thought to the tragedy that necessitated it.
Give thought to the Christ who validated it.

The song writer, gazing at the starry heavens, said:

Thoughts of wonder! O how mighty!
How stupendous! How profound!
All the stars that sparkle yonder
Roll in orbs of vastness round.

But the cross of Christ is more impressive than that—to him who really gazes at it and stops long enough to perceive what it means!

It is

II. A Call to Thankfulness Through Perception of the Cross

Can one, knowing of many to be fed, fail to be thankful for fruitful fields?

Can one, knowing how dreadful would be continuous darkness, fail to be thankful for light and eyesight?

Can one, knowing the tragedy of being crazy, refuse to give thanks for a functioning mind?

Can one, knowing the handicap of a maimed body, fail to be thankful for eyes that can see, for ears that can hear, and feet that can walk, and a tongue that can talk, and a body rich and strong with health?

Can one, knowing the danger of voyaging in unknown waters, when fierce storms rage, fail to be thankful for lighthouses that guide and bell buoys that warn?—and for the harbor when the voyage is over?

Can one, knowing the wasting of disease, fail to be thankful for medicines that restore?

No! Then let me ask—can anyone, surveying the cross, having perception of its stark cruelty and shame, considering the Christ who died thereon, fail to be thankful for all it makes possible?

If we look at the cross and see only two pieces of wood on which a good Jew died—we do not have the key that unlocks the gate to the palace of truth.

From God's side the cross *was* a divine necessity.

From God's side the cross *is* a divine necessity.

From man's side the cross *was* a divine necessity.

From man's side the cross *is* a divine necessity.

From the time when man sinned, he has known that there was something wrong between him and God.

And he tried in many ways to right that wrong—to bridge the chasm between him and God.

Athens, though drunk with the wine of intellectual skepticism, had so many altars and idols adorning her streets that she was laughed at by a satirist who said she had more gods on her streets than men.

In Pompeii, excavators found marble steps before a heathen altar—steps worn down so hard as to make them almost a smooth ramp.

Behind that altar, after the ashes of Vesuvius had buried them for one thousand years, were found the forms of thirty people who fled there for refuge at the great eruption—when thousands found nothing to breathe but flame, and nothing to walk in but hot ashes, and no cover but steaming lava.

In Persia, many mothers tried to get right with God by laying the babies that had nursed their breasts ever and anon by day and night, in the arms of red-hot Moloch in the morning. In India the mothers heard the cries of their babies drowned by the greedy gulpings of the crocodiles—hoping to get smiles of approval rather than frowns of displeasure from God.

And the Jews slew a million lambs on the rock of the Mosque of Omar.

But—

> Not all the blood of beasts,
> On Jewish altars slain,
> Could give the guilty conscience peace
> Or wash away the stain.

Nothing man *could* do, or *can* do, will make things right between him and God—because all man *could* or *can* do sprang and springs from and partook of the nature of bankrupt, diseased, and wrecked humanity.

Can a bankrupt pay his debts?

Can a sick man cure himself?

Can a ditched engine put itself on the track?

Can a man on crutches outrun an athlete who has no lameness?

Can an eagle with both wings broken, and featherless, soar to the clouds?

Can a sick man's moan reach farther than the shriek of a locomotive whistle?

Toplady answers these questions in these words:

> Could my tears forever flow,
> Could my zeal no languor know,
> These for sin could not atone;
> Thou must save, and Thou alone.

God's nature and the nature of sin are eternally opposite in eternal and antagonistic antithesis.

Thus we see the necessity of the cross.

God hates sin so greatly that under his providence the wages of sin is death.

But, while he hates sin, he loves the sinner—even though, as the Word declares, "God is angry with the sinner every day."

If he were to make the sinner pay for his sin by death, he would destroy sinners.

Only one thing, therefore, is left—and that is to have one pay who could not be destroyed by death.

That is what took place at the cross where Jesus died—"the just for the unjust that he might bring us to God.

Perceiving the cross, Wesley wrote:

> When I survey the wondrous cross,
> On which the Prince of glory died,
> My richest gain I count but loss,
> And pour contempt on all my pride.

The call of Christ's cross is

III. Call to Tribulation Through Participation with the Cross

Paul sets this truth before us in these words:

I am crucified with Christ: nevertheless I live; yet not I, but Christ liveth in me: and the life which I now live in the flesh I live by the faith of the Son of God, who loved me, and gave himself for me (Galatians 2:20).

Knowing this, that our old man is crucified with him, that the body of sin might be destroyed, that henceforth we should not serve sin (Romans 6:6).

And that he died for all, that they which live should not henceforth live unto themselves, but unto him which died for them, and rose again (2 Corinthians 5:15).

Jesus did not turn a hand to save himself from the cross:

"I lay down my life."
"No man taketh it from me."
"I have power to lay it down."
"I have power to take it up again."

He set his face like a flint toward Jerusalem and defied and resisted all who tried to thwart him.

He is the only One in human history who went to death as he died.

And if we hear and respond to the call of the cross, we will share his crucifixion.

And:

We are troubled on every side, yet not distressed; we are perplexed, but not in despair; persecuted, but not forsaken; cast down, but not destroyed; always bearing about in the body the dying of the Lord Jesus, that the life also of Jesus might be made manifest in our body. For we which live are always delivered unto death for Jesus' sake, that the life also of Jesus might be made manifest in our mortal flesh (2 Corinthians 4:8-11).

He paid the price for our redemption—to bring us back to God.

A greater price God paid to bring us back to him.

And we ought to be willing to pay the price to live for him—to say to him:

Not for ease or worldly pleasure,
Nor for fame my prayer shall be;
Gladly will I toil and suffer,
Only let me live for Thee.
My life, my love I give to Thee,
Thou Lamb of God who died for me

Dr. Rutherford said: "Men want a cheap Christ, but the price will not come down."

If you cannot say, "I am crucified with Christ," you cannot say, "Jesus is mine."

A crucified Christ and a cushioned disciple do not go together.

An agonizing Christ and an ease-seeking disciple have little fellowship.

We do not have nails driven through hands and feet any more. We need them driven through our pocketbooks to have here what we ought to have here to honor God.

We can avoid that if we wish, but we cannot avoid nails in our pocketbooks and self-will and belong to Christ; and do not delude yourselves with the idea that nickels and dimes are *nails*.

Making a manifestation of Christianity a mere convenience or a sulking in the tent is not giving our hands to the nails.

But, again, the call of Christ's cross is a

IV. Call to Trust Through Permanent Protection of the Cross

Culture offers no protection for man from the penalties of sin.

Education is a roofless house for protection.

Good behavior is a wall which falls when you lean on it.

Rituals and observances of days are a leaking boat for a long and dangerous voyage.

Dependence on good works to save from sins is a silk thread, not a chain to anchor the ship in time of storm.

Human goodness and kindness is a house built upon shifting sands.

> Other refuge have I none;
> Hangs my helpless soul on Thee.
>
> In my hand no price I bring,
> Simply to Thy cross I cling.
>
> Cover my defenseless head
> With the shadow of thy wing.

The only place the first-born was safe when the death angel passed through Egypt was in the house where the blood was on the doorposts—placed in obedience to God's commands. No portals were protective that had not the blood.

The only place where Rahab found refuge for her and her loved ones, when Joshua's army captured Jericho, was in her house, on the wall, with the red rope tied in the window—placed there in obedience to the instruction of the spies.

The only place where the unwitting slayer found refuge from the pursuing avenger was in the City of Refuge—prepared by Joshua in obedience to the protective commands of God.

So only in Christ's cross can we find safety.

But again, the call of Christ's cross is a

V. Call to Triumph Through the Power of the Cross

Many times through the centuries gone forever into the tomb of time has man sought power to make himself master of the forces of the universe.

And he has mastered many forces in his search for power.

One day I took a fast train up the Hudson to Albany.

I thought of Fulton's little teakettle of a steamboat that struggled up the Hudson to Albany in three days—despite its nickname, "Fulton's Folly," despite the dire prophecies to the contrary.

And on another day, over that same route, right up the Hudson, a man flew the distance in sixteen minutes in a jet plane.

Power that masters gravitation, winds, and distance!

But what about the cross and the power thereof?

Is it still an ornament worn about a lady's neck or on a preacher's vest?

Is it still a thing that crowns only a church steeple?

Does it still mean no more to many than an adornment for a church altar?

As a power, is it still not utilized—not appropriated?

As a power, is it still only something mentioned in anthems and hymns?

The *cross* is the *way* to *spiritual power.*

How foolish man is not to use the cross for spiritual power!

The cross is the way home;
The cross is the way home to purity,
The cross is the way home to peace,
The cross is the way home to joy,
The cross is the way home to power,

The cross is the way home for you,
The cross is the way home for me,
The cross is the way home for the world.

The power of the cross works—

Just as electricity in a motor works;
Just as steam in a locomotive works;
Just as gravitation works in the universe.

Those who make it an experience do the most in the spiritual world.

Christ gave the cross its meaning.

His triumph thereon is shown in that five hundred millions of souls who call him Lord today.

The cross was an experience with Paul who said, "I die daily";—and there are ten thousand churches bearing his name.

The confessors and martyrs upset the Roman Empire and snuffed the altar fires of Diana with no weapon except the cross.

Did not the potent cross meet Judaism in the first century—and conquer Judaism?

Did not the cross meet pagan philosophy in the third century, in the fourth century, in the fifth century—and conquer pagan philosophy?

Did not the cross meet English deism in the last century and conquer English deism?

Did not the cross meet French skepticism in the seventeenth century—and conquer French skepticism?

Did not the pages of ancient history become replete—not only with adoration and worship of Christ as the Son of God, but with evidences of triumphs of his cross?

Did not the medieval war lord who lifted up a cross and said, "In this sign I conquer," pay tribute to the power of the cross?

Does not modern history cry out for the power of the cross?

Notwithstanding that many present educators seek to play his deity down to the level of human divinity, notwithstanding numerous organized efforts which seek to revile and discredit him, notwithstanding many present-day functionaries are arrayed against his Saviourhood and Lordship, no personality so grips the human thought, so dominates, so controls, so consumes the human soul as the personality of Jesus.

But, *would* this be—*could* this be—without the cross?

Would, and could the witness of literature, and of art, and of civilization testify that Jesus is the central, supreme, and superlative fact of the ages were the cross left out?

Where but in the cross can we hope for power to stem the tides of materialism today?

Moody knew the cross as something more than an ornament. He gave his all to Christ. And he is still drawing thousands to Chicago and thousands to Northfield almost fifty years after his death. Northfield has a grove of trees at the foot of the hill where he and his wife lie sleeping—with the name of a missionary on every tree, inspired to go by the cross-loving Moody and those who have perpetuated his spirit.

There is power in the cross—wonder-working power.

The cross lifts men buried in sin and brings them up into the light of a new day.

Utilize the power of the cross.

Without it, we are weaklings.

But, lastly, the call of Christ's cross is a

VI. Call for Trepidation If We Pass the Cross

There is no hope to take the place of despair,
There is no heaven to take the place of hell,
There is no cleanliness to take the place of dirt,
There is no justification to take the place of condemnation,
There is no devotion to take the place of devilment,
There is no virtue to take the place of vice,
There is no salvation to take the place of sinfulness, if we pass the cross by—if we "high-hat" the cross, if we have only a passing glance for the cross.

You may blame the Jews for crucifying Christ if you want to; and there is no denying the fact that he died at the hands of the Jews.

But your sins and my sins drove him to the cross—and you were there when they crucified my Lord.

The question of the old heart-stirring spiritual can be changed from a question to a positive statement.

What were the sins that crucified Christ?

Hatred,
Jealousy,
Self-satisfaction,
Self-will,
Self-righteousness,
Greed,
Pride,
Congealed religion,

Concealed hypocrisy,
Pomp.

His simple faith rebuked their parades.
His simple needs condemned their greed.
His love of people punctured their love of praise.
His forgiving spirit made their censorious spirit look like a blot of ink.
And they crucified him!

But the sins are all your sins and my sins. So don't say you had no part in that crime.

He died for the sins of the world—yours, mine, everybody's.

They all together nailed him to the cross.

This being so, the cross calls us to *come* penitently to the cross—not stand afar off as a mere beholder of mere historical fact.

The cross calls us to *stop* with repentance at the cross.

The cross calls us to refuse to pass the cross by. One of the two thieves who died with him answered that call.

The Roman centurion who said, "Truly, this was the Son of God," probably answered it.

Maybe some of those who beat upon their bosoms beholding it answered it.

And the three thousand who were converted on the day of Pentecost, when accused by Peter of crucifying Christ, answered it.

What does that call mean to you?

Is that call as a whisper or a strong voice in your ears?

Is that call as a soft-speaking stammerer or as a trumpet tone?

Is that call a feeble brook or a forceful river?

Is that call as a sparrow's twitter or an eagle's scream?

Is that call a jest or as a judicial summons?

Is that call as a zephyr or cyclonic wind in force?

Is that call the light laughter of a stranger or the passionate plea of a love call?

Are you answering that call by repenting in humiliation?

Or, are you saying, "At some more convenient season"?

Are you just "almost persuaded now to believe"?

Are you just "almost persuaded Christ to receive"?

View such an attitude of passing the cross by with trepidation.

There is great peril, for "almost is but to fail."

A plane came all the way from the Orient some months ago, bound for Chicago—

Crossing the biggest ocean,

Flying above mountain ranges,

Flying over hundreds of islands, and was dashed to pieces in a wreck—almost home.

"Almost" is a tragic word—terribly tragic.

Some years ago a cruising vessel made a journey around the world, and cast anchor in the home harbor of England, only to be wrecked the night before she was going to discharge her passengers.

To the pastor of the captain fell the sad lot of informing his wife and children, as they were spreading the table for his coming, of the truth that the ship had sunk and their loved one with it.

Much of that sad visit remains untold—too sacred for the world to know. But one sentence, wrung in anguish from the mother's lips, has been given to us: "Lost, and so near home!"

Almost home, but lost!

Repent! Repent! Repent! rings like fire bells all through the Bible.

Today that Book urges you to *repent.*

"Now is the accepted time."

"Today is the day of salvation."

Will you answer that call with humiliation and trepidation—lest you pass the cross by?

No man will strut through the gate of heaven swinging a gold-headed cane.

No man will go in on his Masonic badge,

No man will go in on his political achievements,

No man will go in on his stars and bars and silver medals,

No man will go in on his college diplomas,

No man will go in on his record as a soldier or statesman.

No man will go in on his ordination paper.

No man will go in on his pile of money,

No man will go in on his scientific discoveries.

We will all go in, if we go at all, just as we are, without one plea—except the plea of the riven hands and the pierced side.

The cross calls!

I relay the call to you!

Answer not as the fool answereth!

V

Calvary

Christ died.—1 CORINTHIANS 15:3

And when they were come to the place, which is called Calvary, there they crucified him.—LUKE 15:3

Christ died!
So saith the Scriptures.
Christ!
And Calvary!
And *crucifixion* on Calvary!
For that reason, greatly above and beyond all mountains, stands Calvary.

Great is Sinai, sublime in solitude, robed in clouds, shrouded in smoke, illuminated with fire, where, with heaven's earthquake thunders rumbling amid the crags and gorges—where, with the lightnings blazing in zigzag paths across the dark clouds, the law was given—commandments which are not the ghostly whispers of a dead century, but commandments as authoritative today as when their proclamation broke the age-long silence of the desert.

Grand is old Horeb where the bush aflame with the glory of descendent deity, defied the laws of conflagration (Exodus 3:3).

And Hor, where, his spirit ready to wing its flight to realms of day, Aaron transferred his priestly robes to his son, and died (Numbers 33:38-39).

And Pisgah, from whose lofty height Moses saw the land which God "sware unto Abraham" (Deuteronomy 34:4).

And Ebal and Gerizim, from whose neighboring sides the blessings and the curses were pronounced (Deuteronomy 11:26).

And Carmel where God answered Elijah's prayer with fire from heaven (1 Kings 18:38).

And Tabor, in whose shadow and on whose slopes the stars in their courses fought with Barak and his ten thousand men to overthrow Sisera and his hosts (Judges 5:20).

And Moriah where, under the leadership of Solomon, one hundred and sixty thousand men toiled seven and one-half years to build the holy and beautiful Temple.

And tri-peaked Hermon where Jesus was transfigured, his countenance brighter than the sun, his garments whiter than snow.

And Olivet, Olivet of sweet farewell memories, where, with the clouds as his chariot and the winds as his steeds, he went back to God.

But above and beyond all mountains as a skyscraper is above a dugout in height, as a tree is beyond a twig in fruit-bearing, as a cannon is beyond a popgun in far-reaching power, is Calvary.

For there, God in bloody garments dressed, courted our love.

There, at the interlocking of the ages, Christ put away sin by the sacrifice of himself, redeeming man from death unto life, canceling man's debt of judicial obligation by an equivalent which afforded legal satisfaction —voluntarily passing under death's dreadful shadow, though owing the law no debt.

There, with power to smite his enemies with a thunderbolt, he elected to die on a cross.

There, God's eternal attributes emptied their vials of burning wrath upon the sinless Sacrifice in agony enough to make the earth shudder, the sun in darkness hides, the spheres go wailing along their eternal circuits.

There God, the father of the clouds (Job 38:28), permitted him to thirst who came to remove the moral thirst of mankind.

There God, who clothes the valleys with corn (Psalm 65:13) and feeds the young ravens when they cry, left him naked under the sky and answered not his cry.

No wonder the heavens went black and the sun withdrew its light and the earth reeled in its steady course, as in astonishment that love so sweet, so vast, should meet a doom so fearful.

No wonder that all the people came together to that sight, beholding the things that were done—beholding Love incarnate rejected, crucified, tortured—beholding the way in which men treat the embodied perfection of virtue, and then there smote their breast and returned sorrowing (Luke 23:48).

No wonder the rocks rent—the rocks less hard than men's hearts that day—as though shattered that so great a love could find so ungrateful a return.

Earth has no darker sin, history no blacker page, humanity no fouler spot, than that of the Saviour's crucifixion.

> Irreproachable Christ's life.
> Matchless Christ's teaching.
> Astonishing Christ's miracles.
> Marvelous Christ's example.

But all of these would have availed nothing for our salvation had they not found consummation in the cross.

Incidental and collateral all these to the one purpose for which he came—to die, that man born once and born dead might be born again and born alive.

Not by his sinless life was Jesus man's substitute.

Not by his miracles did he honor the law, satisfy justice, meet the demands of divine holiness.

Not by his beautiful example did he take our place under the law.

Not by his preaching did he open a fountain for all uncleanness.

Not by his character did he repair the insulted dignity of God's nature by a reparation equal in merits to the character of the insulted dignity itself.

Only by suffering the death which was expiatory with reference to God, which was punishment with reference to men, did he adequately compensate God's government by an equivalent for man's offense—offer a boundless mercy in terms consistent with the integrity of the moral law.

In death divine purpose of life is revealed. He was made "lower than the angels" in order to die for all. The aim of his life was his death.

In death, he paid our debt.

"The Lord hath laid on him the iniquity of us all" (Isaiah 53:6).

"The chastisement of our peace was upon him; and with his stripes we are healed" (Isaiah 53:5).

The Bible contains the saddest story of man and the saddest story of God. Together they make the saddest story of the ages.

The sadness of the story of man began in surroundings that were perfect.

Man himself, perfect, robed in garments of righteousness, drinking from a life-giving stream, eating from the fruit of the trees of the garden, breathing the breath of the Almighty, was endowed with the power of choice.

In Eden man fell. This began the saddest story of man.

Its tragic color is seen in the blood of righteous Abel.

Its sadness is seen in the shame of a drunken Noah.

Its confusion is seen in the plain of a babbling Shinar.

Its oppression is seen in the servitude of Egypt's bondage.

Its bitterness is testified to in the sting of the serpents in the wilderness.

Its manifold tragedies are seen in the captivity of Babylon, in the sin of David, in the vanity of Solomon, in the betrayal and crucifixion of the Nazarene.

And—in many other things.

But no man can know of the fulness of the sadness of the fall unless he fathom the bottom of the bottomless pit, unless he grope in the outer darkness, unless he weep and wail in hell where race and foam forever the waves of quenchless fire.

If there is no fall, no hell, there is no salvation to preach.

The saddest story of God is Calvary.

Taking its rise in God's love, conceived in the councils of eternity, from age to age, receiving ever new fulfilment, Calvary's history goes.

A far cry it is from the garden of Eden to Calvary, but they have very intimate relations. The tragedy of one is the reason for the tragedy of the other. In Eden we see the beginning of the tragedy which is to end on Calvary, and the agony of atonement for sin which we see on Calvary has to do with the tragedy of sin which we learn in the garden of Eden.

Calvary casts its shadow and blessed radiance from Golgotha through the stormy chasm of human history to the foundation of the world!

And from Golgotha, the place of the skull, to Pilate's court, where, with scourge, they seamed his quivering flesh until it started up in red scars.

And on to Gethsemane's garden, where the roots of his divine emotion put forth their crimson tears.

And on to the upper room, where he changed wine into the perpetual symbol of his blood.

And on to the Mount of Transfiguration where Moses and Elijah talked of his coming death (Matthew 17:3).

Reaching to the Jordan, where his burial in baptism foreshadowed his death.

Reaching Nazareth, where by the toil of his hands and the sweat of his brow, in the carpenter shop, he sanctified all labor.

Reaching Bethlehem, "where that glorious form wherewith he was wont at heaven's high council table to sit in the midst of Tribal Unity he laid aside."

And from Bethlehem, where heaven put out its brightest star to mark his birthplace, across four dumb centuries, and beyond, the cross throws its shadows and immortal radiance—to Solomon's Temple!

And over the victim, whether lamb, or bullock, or turtle dove, on the altar of the Tabernacle.

And over the blood-stained lintels of the Passover night, where the keynote of the cross sounded in the depths of remote antiquity and foreshadowed a deliverance far greater.

And beyond that to the withered garden where despair pitched his pavilions upon the sterile blasted fields of man's lost estate. "And I will put enmity between thee and the woman, and between thy seed and her seed; it shall bruise thy head, and thou shalt bruise his heel" (Genesis 3:15).

That promise, dropped as a sun into man's sunless firmament, was the center, prospectively, of all these constellations which were to succeed each other in the darkness and illuminate that long way unbroken from Eden to Calvary—Calvary, the abyss of the world's greatest sorrow, the summit of the world's highest hopes.

And our text is a sublime paraphrase of the Genesis verse, substituting the language of fulfilment for the language of prediction.

His death, prearranged, prophesied, provided by God (Genesis 22:8), was no afterthought. In words not wholly mine, I say that Jesus was born with the shadow of the cross upon him, that with the shadow of the cross upon his heart he learned to walk, he learned to talk, he learned to work. From his earliest moment upon this earth it was his burden by day, his pallet by night.

Shadow of the cross upon the Bethlehem swaddling clothes.

Shadow of the cross upon the road over which Joseph and Mary, warned by an angel, and in fear of King Herod, fled into Egypt.

Shadow of the cross upon the waters of Lake Galilee—waters placid in the quiet of a peaceful day, or turbulent under the lash of a tempest.

Shadow of the cross on the well curb at Sychar, on the door of the Temple, on sunrise, on sunset.

Shadow of the cross upon Gethsemane's garden.

The cross was with him when they came with lanterns and torches to arrest the Light of the world.

The cross was with him when Judas, one of the twelve, betrayed him with a kiss, which startled him like the kiss of an adder, and burned his cheek like hot coals.

The cross was with him when Annas asked him concerning his disciples and concerning his doctrine.

The cross was with him when Caiaphas condemned him.

The cross was with him when Herod mocked him.

He walked the streets dishonored by its shame.

He climbed Olivet oppressed by its weight.

He rose from the dead glorified by its sacrifice. With those who think such thoughts and speak such words, we agree.

As the mind existed before mental philosophy, as stars existed before Newton wrote his Principia, as this continent lay behind the setting sun long before Columbus thought of a nearer passage to India, as electricity was in the universe long before Edison, so the cross, not an episode but an eternal mode in God's heart, not an incident of Christ's life, not an accident in his career, not a device to meet an emergency, not merely a moral spectacle to exhibit God's love, but a transaction grounded in deep necessity, was in heaven before it was on Calvary.

A sword pierced the heart of the Father long before it entered the heart of Mary. For the cross was a goal in the heart of God from all eternity.

Before time commenced its solemn march did divine love consider man's ruined condition and resolve not to spare the greatest Gift which either time could know or eternity produce.

A love it was that stretched not only over the long centuries of time but through the aeons of eternity—a love anticipating the vast need before it had arisen. God's love was, and is, an eternal solicitude.

Thus, in the cross, the supreme interpretation of God, we see that the agony of God over human sin is eternal—a focus in time and space of that travail which God bears from the foundation of the world.

"Him being delivered by the determinate council and foreknowledge of God, . . . crucified and slain" (Acts 2:23).

"Eternal life, . . . promised before the world began" (Titus 1:2).

"We speak the wisdom of God in a mystery, . . . which

God ordained before the world unto our glory'' (1 Corinthians 2:7).

Knowing the end from the beginning (Psalm 46:10),

> His holy fingers formed the bough
> Where grew the thorns that crowned his brow,
> The nails that pierced the hands were mined
> In secret places he designed.

Knowing that he was the Lamb slain from the foundation of the world (Revelation 13:8),

> He made the forests whence there sprung
> The tree on which his holy body hung,
> He died upon a cross of wood,
> Yet made the hill upon which it stood.

Acquainted with the determinate counsel and foreknowledge of God,

> The sun which hid from him its face
> By his decree was poised in space.
> The sky which darkened o'er his head
> By him above the earth was spread.

Foreordained before the foundation of the world,

> The spear that spilt his precious blood,
> Was tempered in the fires of God.
> The grave in which his form was laid
> Was hewn in rocks his hands had made.

We utterly despair of ever finding any words adequate to express so large a fact.

But Christ's face was set toward Calvary before aught of creation from the womb of nothingness came.

The centuries from Adam to Christ were crimson with the blood of innocent victims killed as types of the slain Lamb of God.

The diversified, systematic sacrifices of the Jews, like finger posts along the highway of time, pointed worshipers to a sacrificial Saviour.

Significant shadows of redemptive entity still ahead, adumbrations of a substance yet to come, by the blood of a thousand altars, these sacrifices, elemental, preparatory, preliminary, rudimental, introductory, pointed to Christ, the propellant center to which the faith of mankind before and since gravitated.

There is a theology that counts such truth too vulgar to be attributed to divine ordinances, but to be viewed as belonging to the grosser mind of man in his unrefined stages of development.

But men libel God and libel the Bible a lie by believing anything contrary to the truth that the bloodstream was ordained of God.

The promise to fallen man in Eden means Christ.

All the ceremonies of Israel's sweetest harps means Christ.

The light that burns in prophecy means Christ.

And—nowhere do we find hope, nowhere find a road to victory over evil in the hearts of men, until we come to

> . . . a green hill far away,
> Without a city wall,
> Where the dear Lord was crucified
> Who died to save us all.

"Christ died."

"Christ died for our sins."

"Christ died for our sins according to the scriptures."

"He was buried."

"He rose again the third day according to the scriptures."

This is the ground of our hope.

This is our gospel.

This gospel, simply and sublimely stated, is our only watchcry of spiritual triumphs in this day when everything for which apostles, martyrs, and reformers lived and died is being whittled away, when there is hardly enough fire in men's hearts to melt the lead in their feet.

This message, which our forefathers preached with rattle of chains amid the heat of the martyr's stake and in the dark of the dungeons, is our message!—the message written in the blood of Christ and fastened with the nails of the cross.

So we must proclaim the cross—that which seemed to be Christ's shame, glorying in what seemed to be the hour of his collapse, emphasizing what seemed to be his defeat.

Preach it, not submit it for subdued discussion in the academic grove!

Preach it, not with piping voice, but with trumpet tones!

Preach it!

Not as epicures in philosophies.

Not as feeders of inflamed popular appetite for amusement.

Not as administrators of laughing gas for the painless extraction of sin.

Not as dainty tasters of intellectual subtleties.

Not as experts in speculative cleverness dealing in the airy abstractions of an "up-to-date" gospel.

Not as dealers in fine-spun metaphysical disquisitions.

But with wooing urgency that lifts up the crucified Christ and warns men of the "wrath of God revealed from heaven against all ungodliness and unrighteousness of men, who hold truth in unrighteousness" (Romans 1: 18).

Else our churches will be lighthouses without water, barren fig trees, sleeping watchmen, silent trumpets, dumb witnesses, messengers without tidings, a comfort to infidels, a hotbed for formalism, a joy to the devil, an offense to God.

By his cross, not by the disquisitions of philosophers, not by the exhortations of moralists, regenerate health comes.

The great salient is that Jesus died! So, for us who deserved death, Christ was made under the law and died under the law; but his death was the "end of the law for righteousness." Made under the law, he bore the penalty of the law, grievous as it was. As someone said, "He arranged his own death sentence when he made the law, and then bore his own fixed penalty in his own body on the tree."

But joy superlative it is to know that the Lord has fully dealt, for us, with the law's claim that man shall deserve acceptance. Legal satisfaction is forever taken out of our hands by Christ. Jesus himself, dealt, in the sinner's interest, with the law, honoring its holy claims to the uttermost under the human conditions which he freely undertook, so that, by faith, the community between Jesus and sinners is real, the community of their debt on one side and Christ's merit on the other.

Yes, Jesus died an initial death, as the Lamb slain from the foundation of the world. Jesus died an official death, as God-selected substitute. Jesus died a judicial death, a judgment death for others. Jesus died a sacrificial death, the just for the unjust (1 Peter 3:18).

And with his dying, the colossal system of Judaism passed away.

Its bloody altars drifted into oblivion.

Its priestly vestments were flung aside.

The ceremonial law, with its mystic rites and interposed barriers, was abrogated.

Jesus took all these rites, types, symbols, to the cross and nailed them there, "blotting out the handwriting of ordinances that was against us, which was contrary to us, and took it out of the way, nailing it to his cross" (Colossians 2:14).

These types are remembered now only to interpret them in the light of Christ's redemption.

They were redemption *symbolized*—the sacrifice offered by human hands. Himself is redemption *realized* —the Lamb slain.

Coming up from Edom with dyed garments, from Bozrah, glorious in his apparel (Isaiah 63:1), traveling in the greatness of his strength, he retrod the way of man's retreat, opened the way to the tree of life, liquidated the bond of inexorable law, sheathed the sword of justice behind the blood-drenched mercy seat. Then God's perfections opened wide their arms repentant sinners to receive!

In all this we rejoice.

For the fingers of prophecy *point* to Calvary! The

incarnation was *preparatory* to Calvary! The transfiguration *foreshadowed* Calvary! Pentecost was the fruit of Calvary!

And as the rays of glory emanating from Christ find focus in Calvary, so at Calvary the history of human guilt culminates, the purposes of divine love become intelligible, the mysteries of prophecy are unraveled, the majesty of the law is vindicated, the great problem of human redemption is solved.

His cross has become the rendezvous and universal resort of the chief of sinners.

The desire of all nations was never found until Christ was crucified.

But Christ crucified, like a divine loadstone, has drawn to Calvary a multitude of guilty hearts, of bleeding hearts, of broken hearts that no man can number.

The cross, the true center and sanctuary of this fallen and broken world, is the only leverage mighty enough to roll off crushed humanity the ponderous incubus which bondage to Satan had placed upon it.

Near the cross, a trembling soul,
Love and mercy found me;
There the bright and Morning Star
Sheds its beams around me.

Near the cross! O Lamb of God,
Bring its scenes before me;
Help me walk from day to day,
With its shadows o'er me.

Near the cross I'll watch and wait,
Hoping, trusting ever,
Till I reach the golden strand,
Just beyond the river!

VI

Worms and Threshing Instruments

Fear not, thou worm Jacob, and ye men of Israel; I will help thee, saith the Lord, and thy redeemer, the Holy One of Israel. Behold, I will make thee a new sharp threshing instrument having teeth: thou shalt thresh the mountains, and beat them small, and shalt make the hills as chaff.—ISAIAH 41:14-15.

In the Scriptures, which survive all changes, themselves unchanged, are many statements that set forth transformations which make the upright in heart to give thanks at the remembrance of God's power—transformations which make the servants of God to "serve the Lord with gladness," to go on their way singing; transformations which make those who sit in the seat of the scornful to give utterances of awe; transformations which give desires for the better to the most debased, their mental faculties won unto admiration.

The desert shall rejoice, and blossom as the rose. It shall blossom abundantly, and rejoice even with joy and singing: the glory of Lebanon shall be given unto it, the excellency of Carmel and Sharon, they shall see the glory of the Lord, and the excellency of our God (Isaiah 35:1-2).

And I will restore to you the years that the locust hath eaten, the cankerworm, and the caterpillar, and the palmerworm, my great army which I sent among you (Joel 2:25).

Instead of the thorn shall come up the fir tree, and instead of the brier shall come up the myrtle tree: and it shall be to the Lord for a name, for an everlasting sign that shall not be cut off (Isaiah 55:13).

And I will give them one heart, and I will put a new spirit within you; and I will take the stony heart out of their flesh, and will give them an heart of flesh (Ezekiel 11:19).

I will open rivers in high places, and fountains in the midst of the valleys: I will make the wilderness a pool of water, and the dry land springs of water. I will plant in the wilderness the cedar, the shittah tree, and the myrtle, and the oil tree; I will set in the desert the fir tree, and the pine, and box tree together (Isaiah 41:18-19).

Though ye have lien among the pots, yet shall ye be as the wings of a dove covered with silver, and her feathers with yellow gold (Psalm 68:13).

Wonderful are the realities of transformation made vivid before us by these words. But these are just a few trees from the forests of God's truth; just a few gorgeous blossoms from the garden of his promises; just a few drops from the inexhaustible fountain of his wisdom; just a few melodies from his harp of a thousand strings vibrant with the consolations of his grace; just a few cups filled from the ocean of his prophecies; just a few gleams from the starry sky of his mercy; just a few cargoes from the ships anchored in the harbor of his love.

Of all the transformations known to man, no transformation equals that which is wrought in human lives by the regenerative grace of God; the transformation seen when, by the power of the Lord Jesus, the human mind is established in the truth of God, the human heart is confirmed in the purpose of God, the human will is possessed by the holy strength of God, the transformation seen when men and women, once slaves to the base and temporal, become kings of the holy eternal, confronting all hostilities without bending or breaking or yielding, invincible to the onslaughts of the world and the flesh and the devil, able to stand against the enervating airs from the south and the fierce blasts from the icy north. What transformations when mere nothings become alive with spiritual power, when the devil-possessed become the devotion-possessed!

That is a truth which makes our text one that is grippingly mighty and sweetly comforting. This text is one of the stateliest cathedrals of human speech. A transcendent triumph of articulation, it stands among the real sublimities of Bible vocabulary. It is a magnificence of language that defies all definition. It is a splendor of expression that leaves little to be added. All the music of heaven is so within its syllables that the whole being thrills at its utterance, mental faculties are awed into admiration, and the soul is hushed into worship meditating upon it. Considering the total effect of close study and prayerful meditation, it undermines like a wave, rends like an earthquake, warms like a fire on a winter night, inspires like music, binds like a chain, detains like a love story, cheers like sunlight, challenges like the call of a trumpet, soothes like a mother's lullaby calms a fretful child.

Contrasts, found in many realms, interest us. Such as the white and the black, the pure and the vile, the fragrant and the foul, the big and the little, the strong and the weak, the fast and the slow, the permanent and the transient. Great was the contrast between Tom Thumb, who was eighteen inches tall, and Abraham Lincoln, who was six feet, four inches tall. Great the contrast between David, the red-headed shepherd lad, with his sling and scrip with five smooth stones from the brook, and Goliath, "whose height was six cubits and a span" and who was "armed with a coat of mail" and whose spear was "like a weaver's beam."

Great is the contrast between the power of shallow rill and a floodtide river. Great the contrast between the speed of a snail on the garden wall and the flight of a pigeon through the air. Great the contrast in power between a cart pushed by a crippled pedler and a locomotive pulling a string of cars. Great the contrast in brightness of a flickering candle struggling in the wind and an incandescent chandelier of one thousand glowing bulbs. Great the contrast in beauty of a lone cactus plant and a garden where ten thousand roses hold up their hearts of ruby. Great the contrast in music of a cheap piano played by the fumbling fingers of a paralytic and the organ whereon and wherewith the master musician builds rhythmic palaces of melody before the eyes of the souls of thousands. Great the contrast between the chatter of an idiot and the message of an orator whose words are flights of golden arrows.

But it would be scarcely possible to find two images in more violent contrast than the two of our text—the worm and the threshing instrument. Look at the worm; a straw can burden it so it cannot crawl. Glance at the threshing instrument with teeth; it can break stubborn stubble into pieces. What a contrast—the worm which the beak of a sparrow can bruise and the threshing instrument with teeth, firm, positive, impressive, ascendant! A worm which a robin can swallow, and a threshing instrument which breaks asunder brickish clods and flinty rocks! A worm which the dimpled hand of a baby can kill with a touch, and the threshing instrument stronger than a thousand mailed fists! A worm which the soft pressure of a kitten's foot can destroy, and the threshing instrument sharp and powerful, which "shall thresh the mountains and beat them small and make the hills as chaff." What a violent contrast! What a vivid antithesis—the weakness of the worm and the strength of the threshing instrument!

And God promises to change the worm into the threshing instrument! Now we need no argument to get us to believe that the commanding word in the text is spoken of a nation. And no argument can make us not believe that the promise is equally and gloriously true when addressed to the individual. God is willing and able to endow the weakling with strength and character by which he will be able to write his services in deep and clear and indelible letters upon the life of a generation. He can transform the worm and enable it to possess a force by which it shall leave its mark upon the fellowship of the race. This is one thing God means when he says: "Thou worm . . . I will make thee a new sharp threshing instrument having teeth."

Let us think of

I. The Need for This Transformation

This need for such a transformation today is seen with the eye, heard with the ear, acknowledged by the mind, felt by the hand, testified to by the mouth. Writing its autobiography in slime, the worm makes it known that it lives in the dirt, because it prefers the dirt. All about us there are people who live in dirt—sometimes making themselves dirtier than the dirt in which they delight to live. Those there are who live in the dirt of gambling, loving the dice of the dive. Stained with the dirt of gambling are the many, from the recess of the school to the roulette wheel of the "house of chance," risking much on the turn of a card or the pace of the ponies. People there are who seek something for nothing—seek to be enriched through another's impoverishment—seek to have an increase of money without rendering any fair equivalent. Like worms groveling in the dirt are many who are victims of the gambling mania.

Those there are, like worms who love sewer seepings, living in the dirt of impurity, living in adultery and fornication, uncleanness and lasciviousness, making many marriage vows perpetual perjury. In our city, as in every city, are young women old beneath their youthful marks of rouge, and some young beneath their olden masks of vice. Behind many are wondrous dreams that lie molding in the muck. Before many yawn the black pits of despondency and hunger and remorse. Women there are unsexed by sin, outcast by their kind, bruised, brutalized, baffled, blighted, terrible toys of love, dirty playthings of dirtier men, the saddest blots that stain civilization. Of course it is not a pretty picture, Neither is it a nice subject. But if the thought hurts, how about the sordid reality? No wonder a syndicated writer recently wrote of a certain woman: "Beauty visited her as a girl and touched her face and figure with an enchanted wand. But there was bootleg whiskey and bootleg love. The liquor was etching her loveliness with tragic lines and her nerves were beating like tom-toms in a jungle. Living became an agonizing ritual. The mornings were blacked out with sleep. The tawdry cocktail bars would welcome her at dusk, and then a blurred evening, and she was maudlin amid folks who laughed a great deal at nothing at all." There is the worm life of dirt.

Men there are, too, who are throwing away in Folly's Court and Carnal Pleasure's Mart the wealth God gave them at the start—giving ear and purse and body to the woman who "hath cast down many wounded"—the woman by whom many strong men have been slain. Many men who have gone after this type of woman—"as an ox goeth to the slaughter, or as a fool to the correction of the stocks"—have found that "her house is the way to hell, going down to the chambers of death." The dirt life of the worm is theirs.

Moreover, there are those today who as to their reading live like worms in the dirt, yes, like maggots in a carcass. Deeply do they dig into the dirt of trashy literature—as worms that burrow into garbage heaps; and they know the contamination that comes from the pollution contained in a vile book filled with immoral filth. Like worms that live in dirt, they are potent in plunging into putrefactions of books sometimes "fairly bound." They need to read and heed the wisdom which Juliet spoke to her nurse when she discovered that Romeo had slain Tybalt:

Was ever book containing such vile matter
So fairly bound? O, that deceit should dwell
In such a gorgeous palace!

Many there are today living—like the worms that feed on swill-soaked soil and sewage, saturated sod, in the dirt of drinking, "drunkenness, revelings, and such like." Taking note of the billions spent for beer and booze annually, we could, with lamentation and cynicism and truthfulness, in some respects label our land the land of the spree and the home of the rave. Many could with tragic truthfulness descriptive of their manner of life, sing:

My country, what ails thee?
Land of the drunken spree and boozer's fling!
Land where some fathers drink;
Land filled with the liquor's stink,
And wine cup's hellish clink
And adder's sting.

Many, with folly more evil than the folly of those who put money into bags filled with holes, "tarry long at the wine, . . . go to seek mixed wine," spending money for that which helps never and hurts ever. The worm that feeds on poison offal is not more in the dirt than those who put into their stomachs that which taints the blood with poison, reddens the eyes with madness, thickens the tongue with gibberish, addles the brain with stupidity, besets the feet with stumbling, befouls the breath with rottenness, weights the hands with fumbling, touches the nerves with deadness, fills the ears with the tom-tom of the jungle, weights the heart with the aftermath of remorse and hastens the soul to the morgue of the morally dead, and turns healthful hilarity into hell-pleasing hiccoughs.

With no disrespect to our country, I say that many, living the life of the worm which revels in the gutter, have, by their manner of life, perniciously paraphrased "America" to read:

> The bottle's foul content
> And wine cup's bad lament
> Is what we choose
> Long may our streets be bright
> With hell's saloonic light,
> And legal liquor's blight,
> Our god is booze!

Many there are who live like the earthworm in the dirt around the slop trough of the hogpen, in the dirt of vulgar language and profanity, with many evil communications that proceed out of their mouths. Many multitudes swearing much and much of the time—and in many places. Vile vulgarity flies near and far with the wings of the offal-besmirched buzzard. Vicious vociferation struts about with the gaudy feathers of the peacock. Foul language as loud as the distress call of the raucous crow is heard on train, in hotel lobby, in office, in store. Vulgar profanity and profane vulgarity, as senseless as the scolding of a drunk parrott, smites the ears of many. Vulgar jest, as repulsive to the ears of the righteous as the hiss of the puff adder or the buzz of the rattlesnake's rattles, makes evil circuit in our land. How pleasing to the devil are many mouths! How deaf are many ears to the words of God:

Let no corrupt communication proceed out of your mouth, but that which is good to the use of edifying, that it may minister grace unto the hearers (Ephesians 4:29.)

'Tis sad, 'tis true that many—like worms that delight in dirt, live in the defilement of profanity. 'Tis tragedy, 'tis true that many— like worms that find dung delectable, live in the debasement of vulgarity. 'Tis terrible, 'tis true that many, like worms that crawl in filth, wrap their narratives about with the stench of evil suggestiveness. 'Tis shameful, 'tis true that many, like worms that feed in rotten cabbage, attempt to strengthen their avowals with assertions that smack of the sewer. 'Tis dishonorable, 'tis true that many, like worms that inhabit spoiled fish, try to fortify their denials of evil deeds by words wholly evil. 'Tis a disgrace, 'tis true that many, like worms which despise carpets and love carrion, reflect upon the sacred and intimate marital relation with remarks which make the pure to shudder. Truly we need to have the transformation set forth in the words "Thou worm, I will make thee a new sharp threshing instrument"—and in the words: "Though ye have lien among the pots, yet shall ye be as the wings of a dove covered with silver, and her feathers with yellow gold" (Psalm 68:13).

We are not straining at a gnat and swallowing a camel; not climbing a difficult stairway and stumbling over the back doorstep; to say that the worms are satisfied with the cheap, with the inconsequential, with things saturated with the soiled and spoiled. Worms do not wear clothes; garments of dirt please them; coverings of contamination they choose. Worms do not care to have place in palaces; houses of clods give sufficiency of delight. Worms seek no bath in clear waters; the pourings of the gutter and the drain ditch are riches for them. Worms do not seek to travel on marble floors; the circuit of the clods, the circumnavigation of the scum-covered pool is the world of glory for them. Worms do not feed on wholesome bread; the garbage pot is their throne. Worms do not behold the stars; the manure pile affords them vision enough.

So also do people sometimes live, satisfied with sordid success, pleased with putrefactions, delighted with the devilish, rejoicing in that which reeks with rottenness, seeking that which seethes with slime, finding ecstasy in pus excretions, being hasty to indulge in the nasty, having no maledictions for the messy, making much of muck, treading always the trails of the trivial. They can say of their lives what Job said of death:

I have said to corruption, Thou art my father: to the worm, Thou art my mother, and my sister (Job 17:14).

And they are as destructive of good as was the worm that caused the gourd, that was a shade for Jonah, to die. And their deeds are as distasteful to those who think upon whatsoever things are lovely and true and honest and of good report as was the manna which bred worms and stank when gathered in excess of the day's need. And, so far as Christian valor is concerned, they are worth no more to God than Herod who was "eaten of worms and gave up the ghost."

Those guilty of living the worm life are satisfied with cheap success, with success in inconsequential matters—forgetting that many things which men think constitute success God never counts at all—never seeming to know that many things we do amount to nothing. When we do not live in the will of God, we do not live at all.

Once Mel Trotter met the greatest checker player in America. Of this meeting, Mr. Trotter says: "He once went over to Scotland with the Americans who went to play checkers. Once when Mr. Hammontree and I were down in Florida, they put fifty-four men in a square, and he played them game after game. Two tied him, two beat him, and he beat all the rest. The next Saturday morning they blindfolded him, and put twenty-five of their best players to play against him. He beat all the twenty-five.

"I said to him: 'It is wonderful to play checkers like that!' 'Yes,' he said, 'it is quite a thing.' Then he walked me off alone, and said: 'It is wonderful, but just think! Suppose I had put the same amount of time into something else! Since I was a little chap I have worked day and night to become an expert checkerplayer. I have spent my whole life in becoming a checkerplayer. Suppose I had put the same amount of work into something that amounted to something! I have never made the world better. If I could succeed so well in checkers I could perhaps succeed as well at anything else.'"

So many succeed in doing the trivial thing—as the sculptor who cuts niches on a barn door but never carves marble. So many succeed in doing the thing that spoils—as the worm that gnaws its way into the heart of the apple, as the weevil that deposits death in the cotton boll, as the moth that corrupts the garment, as the rust that ruins the machinery, as the pestilence that wastes the body, as the derangement that distorts the mind, as the paralysis that makes useless the muscle, as the cataract that dims the vision of the eye, as the dullness that deadens the sensitiveness of the ear drum, as the acid that sets the teeth on edge. "Servants of corruption they—sporting themselves with their own deceivings, speaking evil of things they do not understand, beguiling unstable souls."

But we see in the words of our text

II. Encouragement

For whom? For the weak; for the defeated; for those who tremble at the shaking of Satan's spear; for those who would flee the place perilous and the task disagreeable; for those who quail before temptation; for all who are feverish with fretfulness; for all who are weakened by worry or worn by work or wrecked by wickedness or crushed with care or tortured by terrors.

Let me ask: Are you defeated? Downcast? As a worm trodden upon by foot of man, are you trampled down by some passion, some prejudice, some sin, some something of Satan? Is the devil's heel print upon you? Do you carry scars from Satan's spear? Is your shield thrust through? Is your armor pierced? Is your helmet hurled away? Is your cannon spiked? Is your bowstring cut? Is your quiver entirely emptied of arrows? Is your battle flag trailing in the dust? Is your song of victory turned into a dirge of defeat? Is your sword broken? With despondency you give sad affirmations to all these questions. You set out to cross the river and missed all bridges and were mired in the swamp. You set out to climb the mountain and fainted in the lowlands. Your chart and compass called for a voyage across the ocean—and your ship floundered on the treacherous shoals, or rotted in ignoble anchorage at the devil's wharf. You set out to conquer the land and quailed at the thought of opposing obstacles—complainingly accusing yourself of being a grasshopper. You set out to fight a good fight on the battlefield and found yourself sneaking in the tent or pleased with a playground. All this you acknowledge—with tears, with dread, with shame. But I beg you to be no longer despondent, no longer dismayed, never again cowardly, never again defeated. Because God says:

Fear thou not; for I am with thee: be not dismayed; for I am thy God: I will strengthen thee; yea, I will help thee; yea, I will uphold thee with the right hand of my righteousness. Behold, all they that were incensed against thee shall be ashamed and confounded: they shall be as nothing; and they that strive with thee shall perish. Thou shalt seek them, and shalt not find them, even them that contended with thee: they that war against thee shall be as nothing, and as a thing of nought. For I the Lord thy God will hold thy right hand, saying unto thee, Fear not; I will help thee. Fear not, thou worm Jacob, and ye men of Israel; I will help thee, saith the Lord, and thy redeemer, the Holy One of Israel (Isaiah 41:10-14).

Many, with purposes holy, with aims high, with desire to be well-pleasing unto God, testify that they are beset by weakness. Some who give ear to my words today will doubtless think within yourselves, or speak to me in confidence: "Well, I am the worm. I am not a threshing instrument. I move as a rill; I do not flow as a river. I am a feeble torch; not a brightly burning lamp. I am weak in my faith, weak in my prayer efforts, weak in Bible study, weak in adorning the doctrine, weak in adoring worship, weak in forgiveness, weak in love, weak in resisting temptation, weak in fortitude—a dwarf when I ought to be a giant, am living as a sparrow fussily twittering in the hedge when I ought to be a homing pigeon winging my flight to realms remote, a worm when and where I should be a new sharp threshing instrument." The autobiography of others, written in hesitancy and with blunder and timidity, is the same. It was so with Moses:

And Moses said unto the Lord, O my Lord, I am not eloquent, neither heretofore, nor since thou hast spoken unto my servant: but I am slow of speech, and of a slow tongue. And the Lord said unto him, Who hath made man's mouth? or who maketh the dumb, or deaf, or the seeing, or the blind? have not I the Lord? Now therefore go, and I will be with thy mouth, and teach thee what thou shalt say (Exodus 4:10-12).

It was so with Joshua. He knew he was not as mighty as Moses. But he was blessedly encouraged by the words of the Lord:

There shall not any man be able to stand before thee all the days of thy life: as I was with Moses, so I will be with thee: I will not fail thee, nor forsake thee (Joshua 1:5).

It was so with Gideon:

And he said unto him, Oh my Lord, wherewith shall I save Israel? behold, my family is poor in Manasseh, and I am the least in my father's house. And the Lord said unto him, Surely I will be with thee and thou shalt smite the Midianites as one man (Judges 6:15-16).

It was so with Jeremiah:

Then saith I, Ah, Lord God! behold, I cannot speak: for I am a child. But the Lord said unto me, say not, I am a child: for thou shalt go to all that I shall send thee, and whatsoever I command thee thou shalt speak (Jeremiah 1:6-7).

Thou therefore gird up thy loins, and arise, and speak unto them all that I command thee: be not dismayed at their faces, lest I confound thee before them. For, behold, I have made thee this day a defenced city, and an iron pillar, and brasen walls against the whole land, against the kings of Judah, against the princess thereof, against the priests thereof, and against the people of the land. And they shall fight against thee; but they shall not prevail against thee; for I am with thee, saith the Lord, to deliver thee (Jeremiah 1:17-19).

And I am sure that a consciousness and sense of their own weakness overwhelmed the apostles. But God empowered them and enabled them to light a lamp in Caesar's palace, to carry the banner of the cross over a wider territory than the Roman eagles shadowed—and to "turn the world upside down." Let us not forget that "God hath chosen the weak things of the world to confound the things which are mighty; . . . and things which are not, to bring to nought things that are" (1 Corinthians 1:27-28). Let us ever remember that there were those who by faith "quenched the violence of fire, escaped the edge of the sword, *out of weakness were made strong,* waxed valiant in fight, turned to flight the armies of the aliens" (Hebrews 11:34).

You may say of yourself that you are only a worm—soft, sinfully subservient, soiled, defeated. But God will take the worm and make it a new sharp threshing instrument that beats the mountains into chaff. Beethoven "took the surging seas of tone and made them subsurvient to his rod." So Christ, the master musician, will do with you if you will yield your poor discordant self to him. Angelo, "from the sterile womb of stone raised children unto God." So wondrously will God do with you, changing you into his own likeness, if you yield your stony heart to him as marble beneath the master sculptor's chisel.

The weaver takes cheap cotton cloth and weaves it into a garment which the queen delighteth to wear. So will God do with your beggar's rags if you place them at his loom and let him weave them according to his wondrous wisdom and will.

The foundryman adds seven-tenths of one per cent chromium to low carbon steel—and increases the tensile strength of said steel from fifty-five thousand pounds to the square inch to one hundred thousand pounds to the square inch. So will God add strength to your weakness if only you, as a rebel in humble surrender to his will, let him have his way with you. Then your mind will be established in the truth of God. Then your heart will be confirmed in the purpose of God. Then your will will be possessed by the holy strength of God. Then, through the Christ who acknowledges no mastery in hostile circumstances, you will confront all hostilities without breaking, without bending, without yielding—invincible to the onslaught of the world which cheats, of the flesh which defiles, of the devil who destroys. You will be able to stand against "the enervating airs from the South and the ice blasts from the North."

Carlyle wrote of Cromwell: "Perhaps of all the persons in the anti-Puritan struggle, from first to last, the single indispensable one was Cromwell. To see, to dare, to decide, to be a fixed pillar in a welter of uncertainty, a king among men, whether they called him so or not." And somebody—I would I knew who—commenting upon Carlyle's commendation of Cromwell, said: "And that is the purpose, the office, and distinction of every soldier of Jesus Christ—pre-eminently so in the times through which we are passing. We are to be fixed pillars among folk who are shaking in uncertainty. We are to steady those who are trembling. We are to be strong enough for timid hearts to lean upon." Yes. And this glorious privilege we are to receive through him who maketh the worm into a threshing instrument—new and sharp. In his hands the reed which is shaken by the wind is transformed into an iron pillar which cannot be moved. How wonderful that the worm becometh a threshing instrument. In his hands the shifting sand is transformed into the solid rock. How gladsome the truth that the worm is changed into a threshing instrument! In his hands the frail rope is transformed into the copper cable which cannot be pulled asunder. In his hands the paper boat is transformed into the steel leviathan which dares the dread abysmal deeps.

But we must mention the miracle depicted in our text as seen in

III. Humanity

The Israelites saw and followed the dry path through the Red Sea. They saw and drank water that gushed from the flinty rock at the touch of Moses' rod. The Israelites saw and were sheltered by the pillar of fire by night and the pillar of cloud by day. But you and I have seen a greater miracle—the changing of the pliable worm into a threshing instrument of power.

The people in Capernaum saw the miracle of the healing of the man with the withered hand in the synagogue. Mark says:

And he entered again into the synagogue; and there was a man there which had a withered hand. And they watched him, whether he would heal him on the sabbath day; that they might accuse him. And he saith unto the man which had the withered hand, Stand forth. And when he had looked round about on them with anger, being grieved for the hardness of their hearts, he saith unto the man, Stretch forth thine hand. And he stretched it out: and his hand was restored whole as the other (Mark 3:1-3, 5).

But you and I have seen the miracle today of the puny worm transformed into the potent threshing instrument —when a man, low and obscene, has become "a new creature in Christ Jesus," as Mel Trotter, the drunkard, who said: "When God saved me, he gave me not only a new heart but a new stomach, and through them a new body. When I was converted, I lost seventy-five percent of my vocabulary."

People at the wedding in Cana of Galilee, where Jesus "manifested forth his glory and his disciples believed on him" (John 2:11), saw water changed into wine. But we have seen greater miracles in our day — when we have seen the worm of a human held down by the slightest weight become the threshing instrument with weight that overwhelms all obstacles.

Those who saw Jesus feed thousands with five barley loaves and two fishes saw a miracle of increase and plenty and satisfaction for the hungry. But those who saw Jerry McAuley changed from a Bowery criminal into a great rescue worker who fed thousands and led many to desire the Bread of life saw a greater miracle. They saw the slimy worm changed to the threshing instrument that flailed back and down the enemies of his soul, for in Jerry's own handwriting are these words: "Days there were in my life when I would have murdered a man had I known he had a dollar on him."

Not one time, but hundreds of times; not a hundred times only but thousands of times; not a thousand times only, but ten thousands of times have men witnessed the marvel of the worm transformed into "a new sharp threshing instrument with teeth." Let us look at some records and substantiate this statement.

There is Matthew—sitting at the seat of custom, despised, a greedy grabber after money. There you see the worm. Then turn to the Bible and read the Gospel by Matthew (which Renan, the French skeptic, said was the greatest thing ever written) and see Matthew proving to the Jews by the Old Testament Scriptures that Jesus was the Messiah. There you see the new sharp threshing instrument making the hills as chaff!

There is Peter—avowing vehemently that they all should be offended, yet would not he, saying to Jesus: "Lord, I am ready to go with thee, both into prison, and to death" (Luke 22:33). Yet yonder that night when they arrested Jesus, he followed him afar off. He is either ashamed or afraid to be found in his company. He ignored all that Jesus had done for him, and becomes an ingrate of the darkest type. He lies. He skulks. He swears. There you see the worm. Then look at him fifty days later. Peter has seen Jesus and has had full forgiveness from his lips. At the Lord's command he waits with one hundred and nineteen others to receive power. It comes upon them all, and the noise of it is sounded abroad. And now in the sight of Calvary, the marks of the Saviour's blood still red upon the rocks, facing bloody Jews, angry priests, rough soldiers, and the reckless mob, he stands up to speak. He faces them all without a tremor, fire in his eye, a quenchless zeal in his soul. He charges them with the death of the Son of God. The blasphemer has become the preacher; the coward the hero; the quicksand the rock. Three thousand are swept into the kingdom. There you see the new sharp threshing instrument with teeth, threshing the mountains and beating them small.

There is the Samaritan woman at Jacob's well—meeting Jesus who, "wearied with his journey," sat on the well curb. Poor, soiled, bruised, brutalized, dirty toy of dirty men. She knew many men, but not until that day had she met the one and only man who was perfectly human and yet a perfect human. Concerned about the place where men ought to worship, but not concerned about worshiping him in her soul. A woman with five husbands, living illicitly with a man. There is the devil-serving woman. But she "leaves her waterpot" and preaches Jesus in the village—and "many believe on him because of the word of the woman!" There is the new sharp threshing instrument beating the hills into chaff.

There is Saul of Tarsus—meeting Jesus on the road to Damascus. Bitter as a persecutor, thirsting for the blood of those who believed in the Nazarene, consenting to the death of Stephen, persecuting Christians unto strange cities, becomes gentle as a woman, brave as a lion in storming the capitals of proud empires in the name of Jesus, and glories in the fact that he bears in his body the marks of the Lord Jesus.

There is Moody—the shoe store clerk. Converted, but rude and crude and unlettered. Could not read. Could not pronounce the word "Elisha." But he took one continent in one hand and the other continent in the other hand and rocked them toward God, and hills of unbelief were beaten into chaff. There you see the worm made into a threshing instrument.

There is Carey—the cobbler, just a cobbler. Then a cobbler with a vision. Then a cobbler with an inextinguishable spiritual Vesuvius of desire in his breast. Then a cobbler leaving his native shores. Then a cobbler with a message. Then a cobbler landing at Calcutta on the very day that the French revolutionists tore the cross from Notre Dame, smashed it in the streets, and abjured Christianity. He was denounced by theologians, by traders, by politicians. He was said to be engaged in the maddest, most extravagant, most unwarrantable project that ever entered the brain of a lunatic enthusiast. He was called a tinker, a fool, a schismatic. In India he was tolerated as a toad at first. Then he was hunted like a beast. His printing establishment was destroyed, and the work of years perished in a moment. His wife was insane for twelve years. He suffered from poverty, sickness, and bereavement. Yet he claimed a continent for Christ and opened some blind alleys into endless highways of wisdom. What was that marvel? The worm transformed into the threshing instrument!

There is Bunyan—the dissolute tinker. He was foul of heart, foul of mouth, foul of life. A human worm he—slovenly, slimy, sottish, sensual. But he was saved. Thrust into jail, he wrote a book that climbed through the bars of the jail and walked more bypaths and traveled more highways and knocked at more doors and spoke to more people in their mother tongue than any other book the world has yet known—save the Bible, Book above and beyond all books as a river is beyond a rill in reach. There is the worm transformed into a new, sharp threshing instrument with teeth.

And time would fail me to tell of many others—many men, many women, whose lives—broken, blighted, defeated lives—were turned into triumphant victories of redeeming power appropriately described in the words that depict the worm transformed into a threshing instrument.

We talk about the wonders of the scientific achievement. Science sets forth the wonders of helium. Scientists have sent the thermometer that registered down to four hundred thirty-eight degrees below zero in an attempt to freeze helium.

Scientists have brought forth a new acid-resisting plastic that takes temperatures up to five hundred seventy-five degrees. This is how the Associated Press speaks of it!

A new industrial plastic, described as resistant to corrosion by strong acids and capable of withstanding temperatures up to 575 degrees, was announced to the American Chemical Society today.

No substance has been found which will dissolve or even swell the plastic, Renfrew said. It withstands acids which dissolve gold and platinum and hot sulphuric acid, fuming nitric acid and boiling sodium hydroxide failed to affect the material, which is transparent when thin, white or gray-colored when thick.

Scientists have produced a new super roaster operated by electronics. It cooks everything from green coffee beans to a leg of lamb. August S. Torres, who invented the gadget, proved its incredible speed when he roasted green coffee in one and three-fourths minutes—about one-fifteenth of the time required by the present method.

Scientists also have declared that tetanus toxin, a poison described as being so powerful that an ounce could kill the entire population of the United States, has been isolated in pure crystalline form. It represents the first time in the history of man that a bacterial poison has been isolated and crystallized.

By treatment with formaldehyde, the toxin is transformed into a highly valuable protective agent against lockjaw, and one of the reasons for its production in pure form was to secure a toxoid free from side reactions.

But more wonderful than helium, which cannot be frozen at four hundred thirty eight degrees below zero, is the Christian whose warm heart of love the chilly blasts from a frigid world cannot cool. The worm transformed into a threshing machine—again! More startlingly marvelous than the plastic which withstands acids which dissolve gold and platinum is the Christian, once a satellite of Satan but now a servant of Christ, who withstands the wiles of the devil and the siren calls of the world. A worm transformed into a threshing instrument—yes! More deserving of amazement than the tetanus toxin transformed—by treatment with formaldehyde—"into a highly valuable protective agent against lockjaw" is the man once corrupt and vile but now consecrated to and valiant for Christ. A worm, punily prostrate before evil, now transformed into a threshing instrument aggressive and ascendant.

Ruskin said that if you could send silk threads revolving around wheels with the velocity of light—186,000 miles a second—these same silk threads would be as strong as leather belting. But more marvelous the thing

I see every day and read about every day—men and women changed from worms into threshing instruments.

Let us remember ever and forget never that the power in this transformation from the work to the threshing machine is in

IV. Jesus Christ

He is the light that never fails.
He is the reservoir that knows no diminishing.
He is the guide who never loses the way.
He never strikes a jarring note.
He is never betrayed into an error of judgment.

"Christ, . . . in whom are hid all the treasures of wisdom and knowledge" (Colossians 2:3). So, knowing that, we say:

Beware lest any man spoil you through philosophy and vain deceit, after the tradition of men, after the rudiments of the world, and not after Christ (Colossians 2:8).

And ye are complete in him, which is the head of all principality and power (Colossians 2:10).

"Christ in you, the hope of glory" (Colossians 1:27).

The believer is complete in Christ. Thus we see that this transcendent power—the power that transforms the puny worm into the powerful threshing instrument—is in Jesus, and, being in him and by him, it is the promised and privileged possession of every man who yields his will to the will of Christ. This transforming power makes mere nothings alive with omnipotence. The slenderest wire becomes the channel of the electric current. The humblest slave enters into the fellowship of Jesus Christ. The lowliest worker moves like an archangel down life's plain common way. Every day Jesus, by the Holy Spirit, is engaged in this miraculous work. And Jesus' victory over the world, the flesh, the devil was not meant to be exceptional; it was meant to be representative. It was to be shared by those who follow his leadership. In all things we can be more than conquerors through him who acknowledges no mastery in hostile circumstances. He who entirely understands our nature and every situation assures us that against our foes who look upon us as a weak as a worm, we shall be as new sharp threshing instruments. He who knows to an ounce the weight of cares that burden will give success and strength. He who was tempted in all points like as we are and yet was without sin, will make us strong even as the worm transformed into a threshing instrument.

At a ministerial gathering on the occasion of his last birthday, the noble Russell H. Conwell said: "I am an old man now. I am speaking to some of you for the last time. I will you from my long experience and from the bottom of my heart that the only safety lies in Jesus Christ. Go to Jesus first with all your problems."

Yes, Jesus is the one you can take your deficiency to. He is the one to whom you can take your failures. He is the one to whom you can go for replenishing if the oil in your lamp begins to fail and your light begins to flicker. He is the one to whom you can go for renewal when your hopes seem to become ashes.

In us is an incompleteness that needs God's completeness, a restlessness that needs God's rest, an emptiness that needs God's filling, a brokenness that needs God's mending wholeness, a soiling that needs God's cleansing, an impotence that needs God's power. And this completeness is found in Christ! "Ye are complete in him." And this rest is found in Christ who says, "I will give you rest." And this mending is found in Christ whose mission in part is to bind up the brokenhearted.

And this filling is found in Christ in whom "dwelleth the fullness of the Godhead bodily"—and concerning whom it is written: "It pleased the Father that in him should all fullness dwell."

And, because we know Christ, because we know men and women who are shining examples of the truth that God changes the soft worm—helpless under the pressure of a bird's foot—into the new sharp threshing instrument which beats the mountains into chaff, we songfully say:

When wounded sore the stricken soul
  Lies bleeding and unbound,
One only hand, a pierced hand,
  Can heal the sinner's wound.

When sorrow swells the leaden breast,
  And tears of anguish flow;
One only heart, a broken heart,
  Can feel the sinner's woe.

When penitence has wept in vain,
  O'er some dark spot within,
One only stream, a stream of blood,
  Can wash away the stain.

'Tis Jesus' blood that washes white,
  His hand that brings relief;
His heart that knows our every joy,
  And feel our every grief!

VII

Wanted: More Fools

If my subject should appear as an advertisement in our newspapers—the advertisement put there and paid for by some business firm—it would create as much comment as a smallpox epidemic among doctors—as much comment as a political campaign. And it would create as much laughter or as many smiles as would the following ads:

> WANTED:—A room for an office by a gentleman 20 feet long and 12 inches wide.
> FOR SALE:—Good cow by an old lady with brass knobs on her horns.
> FOUND:—Ring by a boy with Jeannette carved on the inside.
> REWARD:—For return of a shepherd dog by a young lady partly clipped—and answers to the name cup-cake.
> LOST:—Pointer companion of an old man ten months old.
> FOR SALE:—Peaches by Miss Riley—slightly overripe.

But ere I announce my text, let me say that in the power of paradoxical teaching the apostle Paul was much like the Christ whom he adored and served and for whom he counted all things but loss. Jesus taught men to live by dying, to get up by getting down, to hold on by letting go, to increase by diminishing, to find our lives by losing them, to build spiritual palaces on the graves of slain passions.

Did not Paul so teach also in paradoxes? Yes!—because he taught that men should become rich by becoming poor—should become wise by becoming fools. So, to call your attention to my subject and to prove that my subject is not unscriptural, I give you as a text five statements from five verses in five chapters of the Bible.

Let not man deceive himself. If any man among you seemeth to be wise in this world, let him become a fool, that he may be wise (1 Corinthians 3:18).

We are fools for Christ's sake (1 Corinthians 4:10).

I say again, Let no man think me a fool; if otherwise, yet as a fool receive me, that I may boast myself a little (2 Corinthians 11:16).

I am become a fool in glorying (2 Corinthians 12:11).

The prophet is a fool, and the spiritual man is mad (Hosea 9:7).

With the exception of this statement by Hosea, the words of our text are found in Paul's letters to the church at Corinth. In his writings, Paul makes it plain that we can have spiritual results only from spiritual forces. For himself he declined to rely on "excellency of speech or of wisdom" as the means with which to reform and redeem that vile city. Not with "enticing words of man's wisdom, but in demonstration of the Spirit and of power" he wrought there the wonderful effects of his purifying gospel. This he did, he affirms that the faith of the Corinthians "should not stand in the wisdom of men, but in the power of God."

Corinth was a magnificent city. Seat it was of the commercial and intellectual life of Greece. The Greek was there with his love of speculation, philosophy, vanity, pleasure. The Jew was there with his passion for God and religion and with all the attendant ceremonies of religion. The Oriental was there with all his mystic speculations. The Roman was there with his gross materialism and his overpowering desire for world dominion. There was the Scythian, the bond, the free, the barbarian, in one heterogeneous mass.

In the time of Christ, Corinth was one of the most important cities in the world. There the Isthmian games constituted the glory of the world. There, gleaming, gorgeous in the light of the sun by day and in the moonlight by night, was the temple of Aphrodite, or Venus, chief goddess worshiped with a fervor that bordered on the frantic. Each year, a thousand maidens were selected to become the debauched servants of this infamous temple of lust. In Corinth, too, were heard the clank of slave chains and the hissing crack of slavemaster's whip and the tyrannical voice of slaveowners—because there were more slaves there than in any other city of the world in proportion to population. This magnificent city was seemingly covered with gold, since it was given an artificial finish with Corinthian brass, which was of great value. For intellectual development, architectural skill, athletic culture, superiority in navigation, great wealth, unusual luxury, the city was renowned.

To the church in this city went the strange, yet wise, counsel of our text: "Let the wise man become a fool." "As a fool receive me."

And I suppose many called him a fool for asking them to become fools for Christ's sake—for saying, "I am become a fool in glorying." And no doubt many, if they knew much of him, would in conversation or thought declare him a fool indeed for giving up his place as a leader in the Sanhedrin in Jerusalem; for extinguishing with one breath of his regenerated soul his light as the rising hope of the Pharisees, saying he believed in and was going to serve Jesus of Nazareth whose declared kingdom had shrunk to the narrow dimensions of a grave, whose only crown was a crown of thorns, whose death upon a Roman cross was a death of shame, whose open grave was a matter of question with millions. Fool Paul, by the way the world thought. Fool Paul, by the world's standards. Fool Paul, by earth's ways of looking at things and judging things. Foolish indeed, to millions, his testimony, "We are fools for Christ's sake." Rejected as folly his counsel, "If any man among you seemeth to be wise in this world, let him become a fool, that he may be wise." Accepted as worth no more than the chatter of an idiot his urging: "Let no man think me a fool; . . . yet as a fool receive me." Scorned is Paul's counsel today by many. They know not the spiritual paradox: "There is that maketh himself rich, yet hath nothing: there is that maketh himself poor, yet hath great riches" (Proverbs 13:7).

Let us consider

I. The Fact of Fools

The ghastly statistics of war, and the conditions beyond the power of statistics to portray, testify that the whole wide world needs to become a fool for Christ's sake. The ghastly statistics of the liquor evil, the gruesome statistics of increasing auto accidents, the tragic statistics of broken homes, and conditions beyond the reach of figures, show that we are fools until we are courageous and wise enough to be fools for Christ's sake.

The fools with us are too many, because they are the wrong kind of fools. Gruff, gloomy, pessimistic, dyspeptic Thomas Carlyle, once described the population of England as consisting of so many millions, who were mostly fools. Carlyle's percentage is confessedly much too high for the number of fools in England's population or in that of any other civilized country. If we receive, however, the generally accepted definition of a fool—that he is a person deficient in judgment, who acts stupidly or absurdly, or pursues a course contrary to the dictates of wisdom—then we must admit that fools form a considerable number of the population of every civilized land. Yes, we have many fools, but not enough fools of the right kind.

We have the wrong kind of fools, typified by the foolish woman who is clamorous, simple, and knows nothing (Proverbs 9:13). We have with us the fool who is a scorner who will not hear rebuke (Proverbs 13:1). We have fools by the multitudes about whom it can be written: "It is abomination to fools to depart from evil" (Proverbs 13:19). We have with us, as imbeciles who will not cease chatter at a funeral, the fools who make a mock at sin (Proverbs 14:9).

We have with us the foolish ones who know little of the wisdom which is from above and much of the wisdom which manifests itself in "bitter envying and strife," in which some glory, and which is "earthly, sensual, devilish'' (James 3:15). Dr. Samuel Prince of King's College, Halifax, Nova Scotia, speaking at St. Paul's Chapel, Columbia University, on August 11, 1946, must have had something like this in mind when he said: ''The king sin of campus life today is shyness of God. Scientia is often accorded the place of Divinitas. The veneration of science approaches the stage of intellectual idolatry in many of our educational institutions. To the student's eyes it is science, not God, who works our modern miracles.''

We still have with us the fools who despise the Christian father's instruction (Proverbs 15:5); the fools whose mouths feed on foolishness (Proverbs 15:14); the foolish son who is ''a grief to his father, and bitterness to her that bare him'' (Proverbs 17:25); the fools whose mouths are their destruction (Proverbs 18:7); the fools who have never believed that ''wine is a mocker,'' and ''strong drink is raging,'' and that ''whosoever is deceived thereby is not wise'' (Proverbs 20:1); the fools for whom honor is not seemly; the fools like the man whom Jesus called a fool who believed that he had many years to live, when he had not even one fleeting day, and who believed he could feed his soul on corn.

We need fools, but not the kind we have just pointed out.

Let us notice

II. The Fools Paul Did Not Have in Mind

Not the fool that extends an intellectual frontier at the expense of contracting a spiritual boundary—possessing that intellectual conceit unaware of the rattle of its dry bones—that superficial mental illumination that lacks the urge of sacrificial passion. Not that kind.

Not the fool who thinks he can play with sin and get by with it. The man who thinks he can take fire into his bosom and not get burned. Or walk on thorns and not bleed. Or walk amid the contagion of disease and remain immune. Not the fool who thinks he can outwit God.

He did not urge people to become fools like the fool who drinks booze—wasting money on that which addles his brain, ties knots in his tongue and thickens it, poisons his blood—as he forgets that "the wages of sin is death" and that the road of drunkenness leads to moral and spiritual and often to financial ruin. Many mighty have broken their lances on the wine cup and the liquor bottle.

He is not speaking of the fool who walketh in the way of the evil woman "as an ox goeth to the slaughter, or as a fool to the correction of the stocks; . . . as a bird hasteth to the snare, and knoweth not that it is for his life" (Proverbs 7:32 23).

Paul is not counseling people to be like the fool who "provide[s] not for his own, and specially for those of his own house," and in this way "hath denied the faith, and is worse than an infidel" (1 Timothy 5:8).

Paul not once urged people to be the fools who say there is no God. Only the fool would undertake to account for what is around us without seeing the first intelligent great cause! Creation declares a cause that is rational, and moral, and personal, and all-wise, and all-powerful, and omnipresent. My shoe tells me that there is a shoemaker somewhere. I see too many shoes around me not to believe in a shoemaker. I know there is a shirtmaker, because I am able to buy my shirts ready made. I know there is a pencil maker, though I never made a pencil myself and never saw a man who did. I know there is a watchmaker, though I know nothing of watch factories, because I know there is a designer behind all design. I know man did not make the stars and put them in their orbits, nor the sun and put him in his tabernacle in the heavens, nor the moon on her throne; for if man put them there, he could sweep them away; and if I thought chance put them there, I would live in terror, for I would never know just when capricious chance would get rid of them.

Paul is not urging us to be the fools who say that death ends all, for I know that for the Christian "the stars go down to rise upon a fairer shore, and the light is not extinguished forever but relit with a greater brilliance."

Paul is not speaking of the fool who secures gain at another's loss—gets pleasure at another's pain.

Paul would keep us from being as the fools who speak of sowing wild oats as lightly as they speak of measles or one of the unavoidable diseases of childhood.

Paul has not in mind as an example for us to follow the fools who value more the attractiveness of external adornment than the sterling worth of moral qualities—forgetting that while man looketh on the outward appearance, God looketh on the heart and "understands our thoughts afar off."

When Paul urges us to become fools for Christ's sake, he has not in mind the fools who starve the soul to fatten the purse—and get money at the price of things money cannot buy. Nor the foolish who grow rich in the abundance of things they possess but become inert and lethargic in the exercise of all the power of the higher and better nature. Nor the fools who, on fleshly matters daily bent, let empty buckets down into empty wells and grow weary with drawing nothing up. Nor the fools whose most strenuous activity is dancing to the music of self-indulgence by night and in chasing short-lived butterflies of pleasure by day. Nor the fools who are totally wrapped up and tightly tied in the small package of themselves. Nor the fools who place question marks after age-long spiritual affirmations—and substitute a "thus saith the mind of man" for a "thus saith the Lord God." Nor the fools who are content to live without developing a capacity for spiritual realities—and throw away in Folly's Court and Carnal Pleasure's markets the wealth God gave them at the start. Nor the fools who, measuring themselves by themselves, are not wise. Nor the fools who think they can drink the sweets of sin and escape the bitterness thereof—fools who think they can eat the bread of deceit and then their mouths be not afterward filled with gravel.

But let us give some thought to the

III. Wise Folks Whom the World Calls Fools

The world in its wisdom has oft called folks fools who were really wise. Folks who dare to be different for the sake of spiritual purposes and objectives are often called fools. Many insist that we shall go with the crowd. If they break the Lord's Day and we refuse to go with them, we are fools. If they live beyond their means, and we live not up to the pace which certain people set, we are fools. If others indulge in pleasures which, as they know, kill the confidence of multitudes in the genuineness of Christian profession, and we go not with them, we are crowded into contempt corner and crowned with a dunce cap. When a man departs a little from the way of the money-mad, pleasure-crazy crowd he is odd, strange, peculiar, eccentric, nutty—a cranky fool. The man who dares to be different for the sake of spirituality is a fanatic who lives in the realm of bad dreams. Let a man dare open his business with prayer! He is a fool, a religious fool! Let a man walk out in public with a Bible in his hand or under his arm! Fool is he—by some authenticated! Let a man or a woman who are in a group where drinks, delightful to the devil and damaging to the devotees, are served dare to ride the lemonade wagon, and they are placed in the top of the column in the catalogue of fools. Let a man close his office or stop his plow an hour earlier than usual to attend prayer meeting, and he is spoken of behind snickering lips as a fool whose brain cells are dormant.

If some are courageous enough not to march in the world's parade—not to wave the banner the world asks us to wave—not to wear the badge the world would pin on us—he is labeled a fool.

Yet it is the man whose eyes are open to God's truth, whose ears are keenly sensitized to God's voice, whose heart is open to God's love, whose hands are open to the world's need, who maintains a backbone of spiritual fiber and strength to stand up and out without wavering—he is the man for us in the crisis of world or nation or city or community affairs. And while we live in a world where it is hard to prevent the public from doing our thinking for us, making our decisions for us, spending our money for us, picking our clothes for us, we shall be in antithesis to the decorums of gratitude and be found sitting in the seat of the ingrate if we do not have gratitude to God for the wise fools who have made us the beneficiaries of their service.

Now think,

IV. How People Have Been Served by the World's Fools

Anatole France once wrote: "The world has been saved by its mad men." Columbus, by many, was called a fool—and died in chains. But blot out his name, and half the world is undiscovered.

Palissy, by many, and even by some of his own household, was accused of being a crazy fool—and he died in a dungeon of the Bastile. But the secret of white enamel which he made secure for generations following makes his influence felt for profit through the nations.

Henry Hudson made zealous efforts in exploration and discovery, but was "not all there" in the minds of some—and he perished in unknown waters. But he left a record which the wisest of men evaluate highly.

Professor Samuel F. B. Morse was called a lunatic by many hundreds before he succeeded, after nine different sessions of Congress and many adverse criticisms of the press, in getting the first telegraph line built from Baltimore to Washington. But now we write around the world because of a fool who persistently proclaimed himself the prophet of the telegraph.

Cyrus Field, over a period of thirteen discouraging years, was called a fool for proposing to moor the continents together by means of his cable, which was denounced as a mad freak of stubborn ignorance.

And Marconi's wireless telegraphy was at first refused by Italy—because they thought it the impracticality of a foolish fancy.

And the people of Dayton, Ohio, thought the Wright brothers and their sister were crazy because they insisted on trying to fly as fly the birds.

Then, too, the boyhood friends of Lincoln could never understand why he was so interested in books. His interest in books and "things of larnin'" was not to his credit, they thought and said.

Moreover, Alexander Graham Bell was considered, as we are told, a harmless madman with a useless toy when he exhibited the first telephone at the Centennial Exposition in Philadelphia in 1876.

And I read where the wife of Charles Goodyear was the only one who believed in him during those eleven tragic years when he was hunting for the secret of vulcanizing rubber. But on every car we see evidence of his great work.

Fulton was classed as a first-class nut, and his first steamboat was called "Fulton's Folly." But we have the steamboat.

When Stephenson talked of a wagon on rails, pushed by steam, the English people nearly laughed their heads off. But we have these far-reaching and complex systems of railroads today. In 1830 there was one mile of railroad for every four hundred and twenty-eight thousand people. Now we have a mile for every four hundred and twenty-three folks.

Watt was a fool, but we have the steam engine. Howe was crazy; and his first sewing machine was smashed by a Boston mob. But we have the sewing machine today, which lightens the burdens of millions of women.

Many people honestly believed Henry Ford was a fool when he introduced his "tin lizzie"—and a bigger fool when he bought a railroad.

Duryea was a simple fool—but his automobile business became the third largest in the country.

Quite a number of years ago, Langley designed a flying machine, and when he begged Congress for a small appropriation to help develop it, he was the butt of much ridicule; and he died of a broken heart.

And when we read the biography of Jane Addams we discover that she was labeled crazy when she turned her back on society and the frivolous things of life and went down to live at Hull House—because no one was doing such foolish things then. But Jane Addams left a trail over which many travel today, testifying to her wisdom and greatness.

And Jenner, great hero of medicine, was jeered. In Jenner's day there were four hundred thousand people dying every year in Europe from smallpox. Smallpox, with not respect of persons, stalked its way to the door of hut and palace, to the house of pauper and prince. But Jenner found that by inoculating people with vaccine from a cow the great scourge of the nations might be stopped. Some ministers of the gospel denounced him. Small wits caricatured Jenner as riding in a great procession on the back of a cow. Grave men expressed it as their opinion that all the diseases of the brute creation would be transplanted into the human family. Some gave instances where they said actual horns had come out of their foreheads on innocent people. And some people had to chew the cud. But Jenner went on fighting for vaccination until it was found that one doctor in fifty years has saved more lives than all the battles of any one century destroyed. Jeered then!—honored now!

And, as millions know today, Benjamin Franklin with his kite and key trying to draw the lightning from the clouds learned that amid his efforts "our wise Philadelphia fathers snickered on the town commons."

All of this, and other persons and events we could mention, make us to recall the words of a poet whose name I cannot recall, but a poet who deserves immortal fame because of this poem alone:

Thank God for fools—for men who dare to dream
  Beyond the lean horizon of their days;
Men not too timid to pursue the gleam
  To unguessed lands of wonder and amaze.

Thank God for fools! The trails that ring the world
  Are dark with blood and sweat where they have passed.
There are the flags of every crag unfurled;
  Theirs—ashes and oblivion at last.

Thank God for fools—abused, of low estate.
  We rear our temples on the stones they laid.
Ours is the prize their tired souls might not wait;
  Theirs—the requiem of the unafraid!

But I would have you think of becoming and staying

V. Fools for Christ's Sake

I feel that I could appropriately be classified as one who plays the fool—plays the fool for Satan's cause—and be as one who erred exceedingly if I closed this message without urging you to make the decisions and take the stands and pursue the courses that would make you fools for Christ's sake, and make you to be received as fools. Not of scientific fools and inventive fools and philosophical fools do I speak, but of spiritual fools for Christ's sake. And if I did not urge you to become and to remain such until the grave's mouth opens to swallow you or the Lord Jesus comes in the air, I should feel that I had given you a stone when you needed bread, a serpent when you asked a fish, and a scorpion when you wanted an egg. How we need spiritual fools who will point the way and lead the way to the sunrise and noonday of spiritual realities! How we need spiritual fools for righteousness' sake, for Truth's sake—spiritual fools with the high and noble intoxication of spiritual drunkenness—spiritual fools who for Christ can suffer persecution and unjust criticism!

Of the apostles it was said: "These men are full of new wine" (Acts 2:13). There is the higher intoxication of spiritual and not physical drunkenness. There is something that lifts us up out of ourselves spiritually. We then do the impossible. Then it is that the singer, the orator, the writer, the athlete, the soldier, surpasses himself. We catch a new vision, quaff some invisible cup that makes us forget our puniness and limitations.

We need fools like Abraham, who went out under sealed orders to "a land he knew not of"—enduring, "as seeing him who is invisible''—looking for ''a city which hath foundations, whose builder and maker is God.'' He was no doubt laughed at by his neighbors, ''because the mood of the spiritual pioneer was upon him.''

We need fools like Moses who, ''when he was come to years, refused to be called the son of Pharaoh's daughter; choosing rather to suffer affliction with the people of God, than to enjoy the pleasures of sin for a season; esteeming the reproach of Christ greater riches than the treasures in Egypt; for he had respect unto the recompence of the reward [and] . . . forsook Egypt, not fearing the wrath of the king: for he endured, as seeing him who is invisible'' (Hebrews 11:24-27).

Fools we need like Joseph who as a boy would not give up his dreams because of jealous ridicule, who as a man would not yield to the proposal of Potiphar's wife to defile himself with her, who as a prisoner held on to his faith in God, who as a statesman took famine fear from the heart of a nation.

Fools we need akin to the Hebrew children who, when threatened with ''a burning fiery furnace,'' defiantly dared the fury of the king, saying: ''We will not serve thy gods, nor worship the golden image which thou hast set up'' (Daniel 3:18).

Fools need we like Amos who, eight hundred years before Christ blessed the earth with his incarnate presence, hurled flaming words that spoke his convictions in the face of those leaders of state who taunted him and flaunted him.

Fools need we like David, who believed there was more power in a pebble directed by God than in a spear like a weaver's beam when handled only by Goliath, the giant from Gath.

Fools need we like Paul who, beset and hounded by many enemies, was accused of being mad, of being a fool, because of much learning. Yet it was this madman who stormed the capitals of proud empires in the name of Jesus and took the hinges off the doors of empires, counting all things but loss that he might know Jesus and the power of his resurrection and the fellowship of his suffering. He was considered by many as fanatically "beside himself."

Fools we need like Martin Luther who shouted defiance at a corrupt church, stopped not until the corrupt church was broken.

Fools need we like John Calvin who "made Geneva the one clean spot on the continent of Europe"—and who said to the libertines of Geneva: "You can shoot me if you will, but I will fall on the open Bible."

Fools we need like Savonarola who, at a time when the steel-clad modesty of women was giving away and at a time when the people were carrying their priest-hushed consciences, refused rank with the red-robed cardinals of Rome—choosing instead the red robe of martyrdom.

Fools need we like John Bunyan who, for conscience' sake, stayed in Bedford Jail—and though longing for the companionship of his blind child, would retract nothing of the truth he had spoken.

Fools need we like Mary of Bethany—foolish, impulsive, extravagant—giving the costly ointment to Jesus in the midst of a cautious, conservative, critical group. But the ointment has perfumed the air of continents.

Fools need we like the widow with her mites—dropping those mites, all she had, in the treasury. But Jesus so enchanted her folly as to take the two mites and make chariot wheels of them and ride her up and down the highways of the world for centuries.

Fools need we who show kinship to John Knox, who made earthly royalty to tremble and heavenly Royalty to listen when, in travail of soul for the land he loved, cried: "O God, give me Scotland, or I die."

Fools need we who are willing to live on a rigid and spiritual economy, showing the world that they believe that "a man's life consisteth not in the abundance of things which he possesseth."

Fools need we who show that they have in their veins blood like the blood in the heart of John Wesley, whose heart was strangely warmed at Aldersgate, May 27, 1738. Of that day, Lecky, the historian, said: "This day in the life of John Wesley meant more to England than all the victories under Pitt." And I read somewhere this that was said of Wesley: "He left a good library, a well-worn clergyman's gown, a much-abused reputation, and the Methodist Church."

Fools we need like Roger Williams, who was "born with a tempest in his heart." With a mind that was as constantly brilliant as storm lightning, with a manner as unconstrained as the flow of a river; living much in hot water, he advocated "a new society in which conscience is ruler in all matters religious."

Fools need we who—when the world is willing to talk only of "the example of Christ, the nurture of the Christian faith, the governmental atonement, the love of God," all the while showing and stating rebellion at the vicarious satisfaction of Calvary—will believe and declare the truths of the substitutionary, satisfactory atonement for man's guilt, made by Christ to God, thereby reconciling men to God. Today, those who accept Christianity in place of evolution, revelation instead of the authority of reason, atonement instead of merit, are, in modern terms, called fools. But fools for truth and for Christ's sake we need today.

I have heard of magnificent fools. The Willis-Overland Motors prints a little article telling us of one!

"We were resting at our base in Tunisia—a general and I. Abruptly, the general turned to me and said, 'Say,—do you know Chaplain C—?' And I answered, 'Yes, I know him!'

"'Then,' said he, 'you know a man who has been called a *fool,* and also one of the *bravest* men of this war. Just listen to this and see what you think.' And this is what he told me: 'We were fully exposed the morning the Germans began their counterattack at G—. They got our range with their artillery and we had to get into the trenches and foxholes in a hurry when their divebombers came at us in swarms.

"'Just when I thought I had everything under control, I looked down the road and saw some man crawling towards us through the dim light in a jeep. It seemed as if this fellow were coming right out of the German lines.

"'When I got a better look, I recognized him. It was Chaplain C—. His jeep was literally shot to pieces, and two of the tires were flat. Shells were dropping all around him, but he didn't seem to see them. If he did he didn't care, because he just kept coming. He wasn't making more than six or eight miles an hour—but the *jeep kept coming.*

" 'When he came nearly opposite us, I shouted at him: "Get out of that thing and take cover!" But he paid no attention to me. So I stood up in my trench and yelled: "Did you hear me? Get out of that thing, and take cover!" He didn't even stop. He just turned his head and shouted: "Listen, you! It took me eight months to get this jeep and I'm not giving it up for anyone!" Just like that.

" 'I was so mad I couldn't talk, much less shout back at him. But just then a couple of star shells lighted things up as bright as day and I got a good look in the rear of the chaplain's jeep.

" 'There were two wounded American boys in there.

" 'Then I understood. Chaplain C— was being a fool. But what a magnificent fool!' "

But I think Dr. Lorimer, years ago, told of another magnificent fool—a fool for the Master's sake. Hear what he says:

"During my early manhood I became acquainted with one of the foremost preachers of the South, Dr. Richard Fuller. He was a devout, lovable, eloquent servant of Christ, whose story is worth repeating. Born of an aristocratic family, a graduate of Harvard, he settled as a lawyer in Beaufort, S. C. His exceptional ability excited the warmest eulogies and the liveliest expectation. No distinction was beyond his reach and friends predicted triumphs for him at the bar and in Congress. But suddenly every prospect was blighted. A humble minister of the gospel appeared in Beaufort—one of the wandering evangelists to whom our country owes so much and to whom so little honor is paid. The community became profoundly interested on the subject of religion.

"Richard Fuller, to the surprise of all, not only avowed himself a convert, but declared his purpose to enter on the work of the ministry. 'Wherefore this waste?' cried the wealthy planters, the traders, and the gold worshippers; 'why should such talents be perverted, why should they be alienated from the field of earthly ambition?' A protest arose against the fancied sacrifice and efforts were made to shake his decision. Friends remonstrated with him, but in vain.

"The Hon. William C. Preston, United States Senator, a representative statesman and brilliant speaker, came to Beaufort in the hope of influencing him to reconsider his action, and the following interesting account of the interview has been preserved:

"Calling at his office, Mr. Preston began to speak with great warmth. 'Fuller,' said he, 'what does this mean that I hear? Are you crazy? Have you become a fanatic? Giving up your prospects at the bar and in public life to become a preacher? It seems impossible. Let me persuade you to act rationally and give up this singular and, it seems to me, morbid purpose.'

"Mr. Fuller listened quietly, and then said: 'Preston, I was living a selfish life, eager only to win success and have a great name among men. Religion never entered my thoughts, and I was negligent of all duty to God. Suddenly my eyes opened. I discovered God's great love. I saw that Jesus Christ had left heaven and come to earth and died to win my love. This act has so impressed me that, as a man of honor, I can do nothing else but love him in return, and put my life at His service. It does not seem to me that this is irrational."

"Mr. Preston was a man of tender feelings. The earnest words touched him. The conversation continued for some time, and in leaving Preston grasped his friend's hand and said with utterance half choked, 'Fuller, I think you are right. You are the rational man, and we are all irrational.'

"This impressive scene hardly called for comment; but the final words of the senator are intensely significant and may be profitably pondered. Who are the rational? Or, in other words, What is the highest aim in life? Is it the material or the spiritual? Does it consist in striving for the accumulation of wealth, or in something else, and in something very different? According to Mr. Preston, this man who turned his back on fortune and who was destined to die poor, was acting more wisely than himself and consequently would achieve success, if at all successful, immeasurable by stocks and bonds or by credit on marts of trade."

In view of the brevity of life and the length of eternity, in view of the fact that we bring nothing into this world and take nothing with us when we leave it, is it not wise to be a fool for Christ's sake?

I sometimes think that when I meet Jesus, I shall prefer to have him say, "You have been a fool for my sake" rather than "Well done, good and faithful servant."

What think you? What say you?

VIII

Sitting on Doorknobs

As the partridge sitteth on eggs, and hatcheth them not; so he that getteth riches, and not by right, shall leave them in the midst of his days, and at his end shall be a fool.—JEREMIAH 17:11.

And my hand hath found as a nest the riches of the people: and as one gathereth eggs that are left, have I gathered all the earth; and there was none that moved the wing, or opened the mouth, or peeped.—ISAIAH 10:14.

Sweetly sad, blessing my heart like balm, is remembrance of the days I spent on the farm, when Sunday was a day in which no wheel turned and no hoof pounded, except the wheels of the old double buggy and the feet of two gray mules which, as homing pigeon by instinct guided, found their way to the house of God. Blessed day then the Lord's Day, with no plow to make a furrow in any field, with no scythe to cut a swath where grew the ripened grain, with no hoe to cultivate any garden, with no wagon to haul corn or cotton—a day of rest and quiet. Tiresomely strenuous when the foes of fruitful fields made necessary toil that skirted the edges of torture on occasions, when weariness from hard work, lasting from "crack of dawn" till "creep of dusk," made sleep a thing of quickness and soundness when once the bed was reached. Photographed indelibly on my memory is the old rail fence a few miles long which stretched its zigzag course across the hills like a huge skeletonized serpent. Vividly, not faintly, sound in the halls of my memory the voices of hounds in full cry, the moaning of hoot owls, the weird call of the whip-poorwills, the whir of quail wings in startling flush, the raucous call of thieving crows, the music of mockingbirds in full-throated melody, the lowing of the cows, the squeal of greedy hogs, the distant sound of locomotive whistle across the Catawba River, and the hum of harps of pines strung against the wind.

Absorbingly interesting, sometimes deadened with drudgery, sometimes fraught with despair because of drought-smitten or hail-ruined crops, sometimes redolent with melon smell and honeysuckle fragrance, sometimes made less earthly by the visit of the preacher, sometimes moneyless because of crop failures, sometimes made romantic by a girl I knew, sometimes sad because of good-bys to loved ones leaving home—were all these "dear, dead days beyond recall."

Not so long ago, I visited again the scenes of my childhood and young manhood. I preached in the very room in the log cabin where my birth cries were first heard. I heard again the weird whippoorwills, descendants of the wailing-feathered Carusoes of the darkened woodlands I once heard. I listened again to the saucy chatter of the squirrels and the noisy clamor of the bluejays, the great-, great-, great-, great-grandchildren of the squirrels and jays I heard as a boy. I heard again the shrill shriek and deep bass of the frogs whose ancestors escaped my gig. I heard again the mooing of the cows whose sleek ancestors of years ago I had led to the slaughter pen or had driven to the pasture. I saw again the same old farm bell beat its metal tongue against the edge of its brass mouth, as once it summoned us with imperious clamor to the field for toil or to the dinner table for food. I gazed again at the full moon, glowing as in my boyhood days, like a huge white cameo tinged with yellow gold on the sky's full bosom, seeming to be pinned there with star clusters.

Yes, my ears were held captive by voices that seemed to speak out of the past. And my eyes, dim somewhat from the years and somewhat by tears, gazed with sacred fondness upon the scenes of long ago: the old well with its moss-covered bucket, the old trees with their "hungry mouths still pressed against the earth's sweet-flowing breast", the old gates which, while rusty hinges creaked as though in agony, swung open under the pressure of my boyish hands, the old pasture where cows placidly chewed their cuds, the old corn crib which the mules knew, the old spinning wheel once touched by fingers that now "play harps in the glory", the old roads over which I had seen wedding parties rollickingly go or the hearse nodding its dark plumes toward a neighbor's grave. And I looked through one window out of which and through which my mother looked as she saw approach him whose name and children she was to bear. As I looked upon these scenes of my earliest recollection, I was softened and subdued with sweet and pensive sorrow which only the happiest and holiest associations of bygone years can call into being.

But I saw, too, the old barn shed where was a huge wooden keg in which was a hen's nest. It was occupied mainly and industriously by a dominecker hen. She was a beautiful hen. She went around the yard singing, her red comb hanging on the side of her head like a miniature sash. Her love of that nest in the keg was abnormal. She had the brooding, the "setting," instinct. She would hover over anything that resembled an egg in shape or color. Her specialty was a doorknob which my mother used as a nest egg. That old hen, with the diligence of a knight on a long quest, with the ardor of a youth who comes to woo, with the ceaseless determination of a mill wheel that turns night and day with only an occasional pause, kept that doorknob warm, week after week. But, nothing ever happened to the knob. The determined dominecker would sit and sit and sit on that knob. She sat until she looked like she had been taking excessive doses of antifat. But she never gave up. Yet she never hatched a chick.

It was a pathetic sight to see her leave her nest, hustle nervously and cluckingly around for food, and then run back to her doorknob. My mother tried to break her from it. She would turn that old hen round and round and round and round until the hen was drunk. But the minute my mother turned her loose, with the staggering steps of an old toper who was uncertain where he was going she found her way back to that doorknob. My mother would sometimes take her and dip her in a tub of water, but, dripping wet and clucking out some sort of profanity, the old hen went back to the doorknob, hatching nothing.

Again I have seen my mother put two dozen eggs under a hen, hoping for a healthful hatch. Sometimes there was good success and "a full turn-out of fluffy chicks at the hatching precinct." Sometimes a few eggs were "stubborn against the warmth" of the mother hen's body and some did not hatch. In some eggs "there was none that moved the wing or opened the mouth or peeped."

One of these pictures—the futility of sitting on a doorknob, does Jeremiah the prophet bring us in showing us the partridge sitting on eggs and hatching them not.

The other of these pictures does Isaiah, the prophet, give us in speaking of one who gathered eggs that were left, the unhatchable eggs, in the nest, eggs in which no wing moves, no mouth is opened, no peep is heard.

These two statements by God's prophets of the centuries forever gone bring us the up-to-date subject and thoughts on the fact of people who are as the hen—foolish but oft beautiful in personality—which sit on a doorknob and hatch nothing, or of the people who are as the unhatchable eggs. May the rills of thought we present grow into rivers of blessing for all of us! Let us learn and profit by the lesson of "the partridge that sitteth on eggs and hatcheth them not" as Jeremiah brings it to us —learn the lesson of the unhatchables as Isaiah presents it.

First, we learn the lesson of

I. Poorly Directed, or Misdirected Effort

Much human effort is *poorly* directed—and the result is failure. Much human effort is *mis*directed; hence it comes to naught. Isaiah surely had this in mind when he wrote:

> Then I said, I have laboured in vain, I have spent my strength for nought, and in vain: yet surely my judgment is with the Lord, and my work with my God (Isaiah 49:4).

And Jeremiah surely paints the picture of misdirected effort in the words:

> My people have committed two evils; they have forsaken me the fountain of living waters, and hewed them out cisterns, broken cisterns, that can hold no water (Jeremiah 2:13).

The old hen industriously wasting her time and the warmth of her body on an ivory doorknob is a picture of men and women inexcusably guilty of poorly used talents or of misdirected effort. And the hand that "gathereth eggs that are left"—in which there is no movement of wing or peep of mouth—is a symbol of many lives poorly directed or misdirected or not directed at all, but derelict. Such pictures are as grotesquely pathetic as the picture of people planting gold-headed walking canes in expectancy of fruit trees. Such pictures are as ludicrously tragic as the picture of people planting barb wire and expecting grape vines. Such pictures as Jeremiah and Isaiah put before our mental eyes are as full of the comic and the sorrowful as the picture of poultrymen who pull all the feathers from their geese that they might swim with more ease—as weepingly comic as to poorly directed abilities as the soldier who goes forth to battle fully-armed foes with a lady's manicure set.

Once, when I was a boy, some neighbor boys on visit found a huge, thick pasteboard box in our attic. Mother, besieged by our requests, gave it to us—"to make something." That "something" we made, after spending several hours of two days and a few hours of three nights, was—what do you think? A paper bottom boat, a few feet long and two feet wide. We took that thing to the pond with as much confidence as Robert Fulton had in his teakettle of a steamboat which struggled up the Hudson to Albany in three days. With cheers we launched our boat in the old swimming hole—believing it would, with or without cargo, "dare and defy the stormy main." But when that boat, with bubble gurgles that seemed to laugh us to scorn for our confidence in her, went to the bottom, we found that we had misdirected all our ingenuity and poorly directed all our hours of toil. We duplicated the picture of the old hen sitting on the doorknob. We duplicated the picture of him who "gathereth eggs that are left"—in which no wing moves, no mouth peeps!

All this forms a portrait of men and women who go through life—busy at this, busy at that, busy at the other, busy at the minor but never busy at the things that matter most. Here is a man who is busy at the lodge and at business, but never at the church. Is he not, when it comes to matters spiritual, the hen (or rooster) on a doorknob? Here is a man who is busy at golf, or other sports,—but never at God's work of "visiting the fatherless or widows." Is he not, when it comes "to the help of the Lord against the mighty," as "eggs that are left" in the hand of him who hopeth for a hatch? In the shadow of the brevity of life, in the light of the swiftness of time and the length of eternity—is he not guilty of poorly directed effort?

Here is a woman who has time to learn the latest dance steps, time for the bridge club and book club, time for the lodges, time for the movies, time for the D.A.R., time for various activities, but no time—or little time—for the prayer meeting, the missionary society, the church. In thinking upon things that matter most and weigh heaviest on God's sales and measure highest by God's measuring rod, is she not guilty of poorly directed effort and blundering use of talents and personality? Is she not, whether she be a young woman or an old woman, "as the partridge which sitteth on eggs and hatcheth them not"? Is not the hand that gathered the eggs that are left—eggs in which no life is—an appropriate symbol of her misused life?

Once, years ago, I found this in a book and copied it. The name of the book and the author I have forgotten! But hear ye—remembering that if you rebuke a wise man he will love you:

"Most Americans have become perpetual joiners in a desperate effort to escape from the obscurity of mediocrity. By the time your ordinary garden variety of a common citizen attains the age of fifty, he has collected a whole trunkful of insignia, robes, turbans, coats, caps, embroideries, buckles, medals, pins, which he has acquired in his poorly directed effort. He has joined the Moose, and the Masons, the Odd Fellows and the Elks, the Red Men and the Eagles, the Owls and the Reindeers, the Pelicans and the Mystic Knights of the Sea—until his breast is covered with badges and his hand is calloused with mystic grips and his voice hoarse with whispered countersigns. He finds no inconsistency in joining one hundred different lodges and in racing the calendar in the vain hope of squeezing in an extra lodge night each week or so. Instead of being himself he becomes a potpourri of brotherhoods and fellowships—and lots of times to the exclusions of the activities and fellowships of the church. Poorly directed effort! A doorknob sitter—often is he. The insatiable joiner of societies is a doorknob sitter. He belongs to so many things that nothing belongs to him. His waistcoat bulges with cryptic badges while he dashes around like an alderman at a funeral. Energy shoots from him in sparks, and like Aesop's fly on the axle, he sees the mighty dust he raises. In a world of uncounted surprises he may join so many dinner clubs, secret orders, associations, brotherhoods, unions, and sister alliances that the sheriff will not find him when he comes to give notice of foreclosure on the furniture."

Be he lawyer, be he physician, be he merchant, be he preacher, he may think that many memberships in many organizations will hatch him out much trade and much success and many real friends and get a yardful of the chickens of opportunity. But is that the case? We all know that fraternities and clubs can serve a useful purpose, but one can squander potential sovereignty and much energy on "eggs that do not hatch"—on "eggs that are left in which there is no wing to flutter or voice to peep" as evidence of spiritual life and power and success.

But, penetrating to the very heart of our text, we learn the lesson of

II. Speed in the Wrong Direction

That old industrious hen of my boyhood days I shall long remember. She gave me the lesson of speed in the wrong direction—of motion which arrives nowhere out of breath—of movement that ends in futile frustration. Quick was the old hen to get back to the nest in the wooden keg, hurrying flutteringly and cluckingly along, after spending a few grudging minutes in eating. With evident reluctance, she left her "throne in the keg" to gulp down a few grains of corn and to wet her dry throat at the water pan at the stable door. But always she scurried back, her stiff wings helping her stiffer feet along, with a sort of hen elation expressing itself in every step and in her settling down again in the keg. Speedy old hen—making haste to sit on a doorknob. Determinedly moving hen—hurrying to spend the day and the night on something and at something fruitlessly futile—on a doorknob, ensconced in hay, wherein "there was none that moved the wing and opened the mouth or peeped."

You cannot grind corn with water that has gone over the dam. You cannot heat a house with last year's fire. You cannot make engagements on a last year's calendar. You cannot get anywhere going in a circle. The old Negro was wise, though loving, in his rebuke to his wife who spent one dollar on the merry-go-round when the circus was in town. To her, after she has finished "riding out" the sum of one dollar, he said: "Now, you done spent dat dollar—and you aint git no whar an' you aint been no whar yit."

No, you cannot get anywhere journeying in a circle. And you cannot reach the harbor going round and round the harbor. And you cannot avoid the rocks when making speed toward the rocks. In baseball parlance, you cannot hit home runs knocking fouls behind the catcher.

You cannot reach the attic going down steps that lead to the cellar.

Some years ago, the young Mr. Reigel, quite a football player, dimmed his stardom in the Rose Bowl. In the football game between Georgia Tech and California he speedily ran the whole length of the football field—carrying the ball the while—while thousands gasped in utter dismay, and Graham McNamee wildly shouted: "He's gone crazy—surely." Yes, he ran one hundred yards. But the trouble—the trouble that brought his team defeat—was that he ran that distance in the wrong direction—the direction that was against and not in behalf of the fortunes of his team.

Some, running with a multitude to do evil, are moving speedily in the wrong direction; toward drunkenness, not sobriety; toward the barroom and tavern, not to the altar and pew of God's house; toward shame and dishonor, not honor; toward the pits of putridity, not toward the peaks of purity; toward the foul, not the fragrant; toward the spiritually skimpy, not the spiritually sufficient; toward the false, not the true; toward the penitentiary of fear, not the place of peace; toward that which is ghoulishly degrading, not that which is elevating in godliness; toward hell, not heaven. Many make haste with feet that run not in paths of righteousness.

The Pyramid of Cheops is composed of more than two million blocks of stone—each block weighing an average of fifty thousand pounds—covering at the base thirteen acres, rising to a height of nearly five hundred feet. It has an immensity overwhelming. It took one hundred thousand men twenty years to build it. But it is only a dead monument to a dead king! What an illustration of poorly directed and misdirected effort—of movement in a direction that ended as eggs that have not life and hatch nothing as evidence of life.

Then, too, in our text we learn the lesson of

III. Riches Gotten by Wrong Methods

We read in the Book, which is not like any other book in its claims:

Treasures of wickedness profit nothing: but righteousness delivereth from death (Proverbs 10:2).

We read in the Bible—Book unlike all other books in its message, claims, and moral tone:

There is that maketh himself rich, yet hath nothing: there is that maketh himself poor, yet hath great riches (Proverbs 13:7).

We read in the Book, which is regenerate in power, these words from the author of our text:

Woe unto him that buildeth his house by unrighteousness, and his chambers by wrong; that useth his neighbour's service without wages, and giveth him not for his work (Jeremiah 22:13).

We read in the Book, which is so harmonious in infinite complexity:

Ye have sown much, and bring in little; ye eat, but ye have not enough; ye drink, but ye are not filled with drink; ye clothe you, but there is none warm; and he earneth wages earneth wages to put it into a bag with holes (Haggai 1:6).

We read in the Book, which is inspired in totality and so personal in application, the words of Jesus:

Take heed, and beware of covetousness: for a man's life consisteth not in the abundance of the things which he possesseth (Luke 12:15).

The important thing is to live rich, not die rich—to live as spiritual millionaires, not to die leaving the record that millions was all we were worth. Are we here mainly to make a living? No. Our business is to make a life. Many have made a living who never made a life. Too many live as though the most worthy ambition was to accumulate. Yet they have never possessed their possessions—their possessions possess them. They do not master their money and make it a servant. They let their money master them—and become a tyrant. Yet no man wants the final judgment on himself to be based on what he got—to be foundationed on his pocketbook. Unless a man has poor ideas of real values, he wants people to read in his obituary not a balance sheet of his wealth but a story of his service to humanity.

I do not know that Alexander the Great ever read after Isaiah or Jeremiah, but he said something with his dying breath which is in agreement with the tragedy set forth in our text! He said: "Thrust my hands through my shroud that the world may see that they are empty."

We need to listen to the words of my old Bible teacher in Furman University, who said. "All you will hold in your cold dead hand is what you gave away."

Wise the words of a father who said: "If I teach my boy to work, he will not need any money I can leave him. If I do not teach him to work, no money that I can leave him will help any!" Let us remember that many of those who have enriched the world have not been rich in this world's goods. Sir Isaac Newton was not. Elijah was not. Nor Herschel. Nor Columbus. Nor Fulton. Nor Jefferson. Nor Lincoln. Nor Pasteur. Nor Moody. Nor Grenfell. Nor Russell Conwell.

Abraham of Bible chronicle was rich—rich in cattle, in silver, in gold; but that is not wherein his immortal renown lies. Moses had the chance to be rich, but he scorned it as one scorns a bed offered by the murderer of one's mother. Job was rich; but his patience in frightful afflictions and his faith in God when he, through lips that were rotten with disease, voiced the anguish of generations, is what we think upon when we think of Job. John Hancock of Massachusetts was a very rich man in America when the Revolutionary War broke out. But that fact is hardly known except by a few historians who make a specialty of unimportant information. And Jesus, who has enriched all lands and bannered continents with love, had no pocketbook but the mouth of a fish, gave up the riches of heaven for earthly poverty that we, through his poverty, might lay hold upon the wealth of eternal life and the riches of heaven.

Those who spend time and talent in doing nothing but laying up treasure on earth shall, in matters spiritual, bequeath to posterity no more than the old hen who gave her all to the hatching of a doorknob—and got nothing.

Give ear again just here to Jeremiah:

The heart is deceitful above all things, and desperately wicked: who can know it? I the Lord search the heart, I try the reins, even to give every man according to his ways, and according to the fruit of his doings. As the partridge sitteth on eggs, and hatcheth them not; so he that getteth riches, and not by right, shall leave them in the midst of his days, and at his end shall be a fool (Jeremiah 17:9-11).

Ponder again what Isaiah hath written:

And my hand hath found as a nest the riches of the people: and as one gathered eggs that are left, have I gathered all the earth; and there was none that moved the wing, or opened the mouth, or peeped. Shall the ax boast itself against him that heweth therewith? or shall the saw magnify itself against him that shaketh it? as if the rod should shake itself against them that lift it up, or as if the staff should lift up itself, as if it were no wood. Therefore shall the Lord, the Lord of hosts, send among his fat ones leanness; and under his glory he shall kindle a burning like the burning of a fire (Isaiah 10: 14-16).

This text presents to us also the lesson of

IV. Time Wasted

The old hen, leaving that doorknob only a few minutes at a time to gobble a little food cluckingly, wasted much time trying to get a chick from that lifeless piece of ivory. The partridge sitting on eggs that did not hatch grew daily older with time used for naught. The man putting his hand in the nest to gather the eggs that were left only to find them lifeless—with no wing to move and no mouth to peep—found out that one million minutes so used brought no profit.

We need to learn the meaning of moments. Some years ago it was discovered that between the sun's time as recorded at Greenwich and as recorded at Paris there was the difference of one-sixteenth of a second. To find that infinitesimal particle of time, considerably less than the "twinkingly of an eye," great expense was incurred. In Paris a special building was constructed, costly instruments were installed, and high-salaried mathematical experts were engaged. Now you say, "That was all nonsense." By no means! Those astronomers were engaged in a very important task; for longitude, which is calculated at Greenwich time, determines the boundaries of many countries, and even a slight variation in longitude would cause very serious trouble.

Human destiny is determined by small particles of time. Many moments that are ours are momentous moments.

Napoleon, called the archangel of war, but who died a chained Prometheus on lonely St. Helen's Isle, the world exultant at his fall, usually seized the moment in its flight and charged it through and through with the life of action. After the passage of arms at Reichenback, which cost him Duroc, he moodily said to Caulaincourt's appeal for orders: "Tomorrow—everything!" Multitudes of young people are disposed to answer the serious claims on them for earnest work by saying—by word or by attitude—"Tomorrow, everything." They forget that it hurts less to be tired than bored. Foolish are the youth who waste pity on the youth who is compelled to work. Young people who do not throw their whole souls into the doing of a worthy task fail to see that they will find in every tomorrow only what they impart from today.

Tom Hood said: "My forty years have been forty thieves; for they have stolen strength, hope, and many joys." Let not that be your sad lament, young people, when you get to that age.

Somebody said "Time is what we want most and use the worst." There are those who say, "I have no time to live in the world's strife like a hero." But you will have time to have the frightful remorse of not having done so. "I have no time to avail myself of that opportunity," say some with self-pity. But you will have time to regret; for opportunity is easier to grasp by the forelock than by the heel.

"I have no time to attempt to lead young people to saving and serving faith in Christ," say some, busily excusing themselves. But unless your eyes be glass and your heart be marble, you will have time to weep over their follies and transgressions—or smug and haughty self-righteousness.

"I have no time to lay such a foundation as some wise preachers talk about," say others—as those who prefer the shadow to the substance. But they will have time to see the whole house fall and the foundation swept away.

"We have no time to put oil in our lamps!" exclaim some who forget that laziness is the lever that lifts nothing. But they will have time, in a midnight of despair, to cry out in fearful unreadiness "when the bridegroom comes."

"We have no time to mend the faulty link in the anchor chain", carelessly say some, with evident irritation when the claims of Christ are placed upon their hearts. But they will have time to hear the chain snap at the place of the faulty link—and time to see the ship begin to toss or drift without anchor.

"We have no time to study and walk in companionship with good books on the intellectual road," silly chime some, with clownish grin—in the presence of schools and libraries. But they will have time to be disgusted with the spiders of ignorance and little learning spinning their webs throughout the mental house.

"We have no time to get ready to meet God," say some scoffingly, as those who scorn the warnings of God as though they were idiotic chatter. But they will have time to stand before him naked of soul, and ashamed and afraid.

Moreover, in our text we do not have to search as one searcheth in a rag pile for a scrap of silk to find the lesson of

V. No Returns

The partridge which Jeremiah pictures as sitting on eggs that do not hatch got no returns from all her work. The hand Isaiah pictures as gathering "eggs that are left" after the hatching of the other eggs in the nest as nothing in returns when full of "the eggs that are left"—for "there was none that moved the wing, or opened the mouth or peeped." No returns as rewards for labor expended and time spent. No dividends declared, even after many days go by. No interest to accrue from what is invested.

Are you finding any real joy in gathering "eggs that are left"? Are you attempting to get chicks from a doorknob? Are you hoping for spiritual hatchings from carnal eggs? Are you spending time with the devil's doorknob—placed in a comfortable business nest? If you get chicks from a doorknob or from eggs that respond not to the brooding heat of the hen's body, you will do what no hen has ever done.

In the *Universal Engineer* we find this in praise of the hen:

Hard work means nothing to a hen. She just keeps on digging worms and laying eggs regardless of what the business prognosticators say about the outlook for this or any other year.

If the ground is hard, she scratches harder. If it's dry, she digs deeper. If it's wet, she digs where it's dry. If she strikes a rock, she works around it. If she gets a few more hours of daylight, she gives us a few more eggs.

But always she digs up worms and turns them into hard-shelled profits as well as tender, profitable broilers. Did you ever see a pessimistic hen? Did you ever hear of one starving to death waiting for worms to dig themselves to the surface?

Did you ever hear one cackle because work was hard?

Not on your life! They save their breath for digging and their cackles for eggs.

But, though success means digging, though we praise the hen for being industrious, we cannot commend the hen for hatching chicks from doorknobs—because that just isn't done. The attractive advertisement that appeared for years with the words, "Hasn't scratched yet," can be changed a bit and applied to doorknobs and eggs without fertility: "Hasn't hatched yet."

There are no returns for God or humanity from ungodly houses. There are no returns for God in wrong ambitions. There are no returns for God from an evil heart. There are no returns for God in the sordid and sinful life.

Learn from the hen on the doorknob the futility of all efforts for happiness and power in those who seek pleasures in the pursuit of lower things. Some say: "Eat, drink, and be merry, for tomorrow we die!" Unfortunately for society some prodigals do not die tomorrow. They live. And they continue to live after they have squandered their substance, requiring to be supported by their relatives or at the poor farm. Many an Esau does not die soon enough for his own happiness or that of other people. Their useless hulks float menacingly up and down the seas long after they have ceased to carry any helpful cargo.

The artist Barton, who had full page cartoons in *Life* and *Liberty* and *Puck,* took his own life. Before he went, here is what he wrote, as he died at forty:

I have run from wife to wife, from house to house, and from country to country in a ridiculous effort to escape from myself. In doing so I am very much afraid I have caused a great deal of unhappiness to those who have loved me.

In particular my remorse is bitter over my failure to appreciate my beautfiul lost angel— Carlotta—the only woman I ever loved and whom I respect and admire most of all. She is the one person who could have saved me, had I been saveable. She did her best. I hope that she will understand and forgive me a little.

No one thing is responsible for this and no one person —except myself. If gossip insists upon something more definite and thrilling as a reason, let us choose my pending appointment with my dentist or the fact that I am painfully short of cash.

I've done it because I am fed up with inventing devices for getting through 24 hours a day and with bridging over a few months, periodically, with some artificial interests such as a new gal, who unnerves me to the point where I forget my own troubles.

I present the remains, with my compliments, to any medical school that fancies them—or soap can be made of them. In them I haven't the slightest interest except that I want them to cause as little bother as possible.

He made life a thing of sitting on doorknobs. Happiness and peace never hatched out. Nothing of real beauty and spiritually came to him. Those who find pleasure in the pursuits of lower things are sitting on doorknobs. Animals act entirely from instinct alone, and we call them nonmoral. When people act from instinct alone, they become immoral. And immorality is always a failure.

The way of life has been pictured as a "straight and narrow" one. It is that. Thank God it is that. Thank God he has not left us in the dark as to that in the truth of his Bible. It is that, but it is something more than that, too. It is a glorious way. It has sudden lights that brighten it. It is overhung by the mercy of God. It is traveled by fellow mortals who are really trying. It ends in completion of character and in eternal life. Any other way of living is as futile to living what the human and life need most—in life, in death, in time, in eternity—as the old hen's attempt to bring forth a family of live and lively chicks from a dead doorknob. Any other way of living is as impotent to bring the joy ever rich and abiding as expecting chickens from rotten eggs "where there was no one that moved the wing, or opened the mouth or peeped."

Lee, Robert G. 252.
Pulpit Pleadings 06
LEE